My Side of the River

REFLECTIONS OF A CATSKILL FLY FISHERMAN

Roger Menard

Illustrations by David Taft

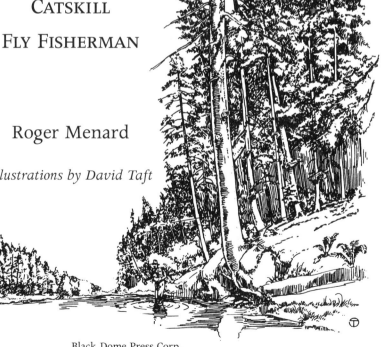

Black Dome Press Corp.
1011 Route 296, Hensonville, New York 12439
Tel: (518) 734-6357 Fax: (518) 734-5802 www.blackdomepress.com

Published by
Black Dome Press Corp.
1011 Route 296
Hensonville, New York 12439
www.blackdomepress.com
Tel: (518) 734-6357 Fax: (518) 734-5802

First Edition

Library of Congress Cataloging-in-Publication Data:

Menard, Roger.
  My side of the river : reflections of a catskill fly fisherman / by
Roger Menard.-- 1st ed.
     p. cm.
  ISBN 1-883789-32-X (trade paper)
  1. Fly fishing--New York--Catskill Mountains--Anecdotes. 2. Menard,
Roger. I. Title.
  SH529 .M45 2002
  799.1'24'0974738--dc21
                                                      2002019612

Photography by Roger and Lisa Menard.
Design by Carol Clement, Artemisia, Inc.
Printed in the USA

Dedicated ... with love
to Lisa, my wife and best friend.
R.M.

Roger Menard

Acknowledgments

Special thanks to Lisa, my wife and inspiration, who spent hours reading and re-reading countless manuscript versions of this book; to artist and angler Dave Taft, whose artwork graces the pages of this book; to the "Woodstock anglers" for many seasons of fine food and friendship; to Debbie Allen and Steve Hoare at Black Dome Press for their easy manner and help with the preparation of this book; to proofreaders Larry Bauer, Matina Billias, and Ed Volmar for their keen eyes and valued suggestions; and to Carol Clement, whose layout and graceful design of this book complements its spirit.

And finally, a special tribute to all of those trout and salmon who for more than five decades came to my flies, and to those who didn't, for it was they who taught me a lesson in humility and kept me coming back.

Lisa Menard

Contents

Acknowledgments   5

Prologue   10

Random Casts: A Preface   13

Mecca   19

Opening Day   25

First Impressions   29

Small Streams   35

Quill Gordons and Hendricksons   45

Hatfish on the Esopus   53

Cane   63

Some Thoughts on Feathers   73

More Feathers   81

Endangered Species   87

Brook Trout: Medicine Places   91

Along The Way   101

The Unexplained   107

The Quest   119

Blueberry Trout   125

Autumn Landlocks   131

A Full Creel   139

Appendix: Getting Started   145

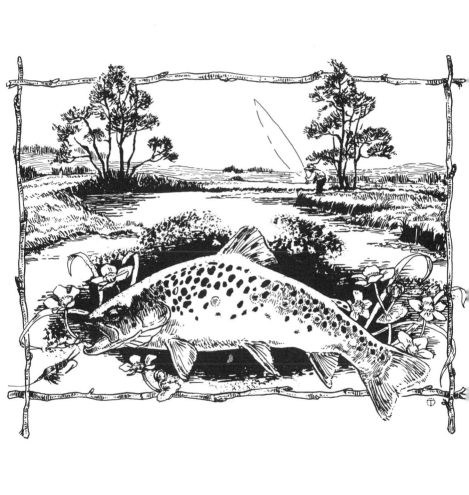

Prologue

Frank Mele was an excellent musician, teacher, and author. He was a gracious angling companion and a very dear friend. Several months before his passing he sent me the following prologue sharing our love for the brook trout: *Salvelinus Fontinalis*, "the little salmon of the fountain."

God had just created
the Garden of Eden
and He saw it was good.
Then God created Adam,
saw this creation was also good
and said to him:
"What do you wish
for your life's quest
in joyfulness?"

"Living jewels," replied Adam.
"Jewels that dart like wraiths
in sunlight and shadow."

"Very good," said God, adding,
"Before then I must make
the first jewel."
Straightway a brooklet appeared
and began to dance the bubbles
that broke into song.

Then Adam remembered the rod
leaning against the trunk
of a Garden tree and said, "What,
God, could that be?"

"That," said God, "is a fly rod
with which to weave
a spell in your quest. And now
I will make your other living jewel."
Straightway Adam saw
a quick movement in the pool and saw
it was another living jewel.
"What do you call him?" asked Adam.

"That," said God
"is the brook trout.
Perhaps I am risking immodesty if I say
he is one of my masterpieces."
"And," continued God, "you will find him
in the joyous little rivers
and the purest ponds and lakes where,
as here, I painted his back the dark blue
of the night. On his sides I sprinkled
the freckles of the starry sky;
at his fins I brushed in
the colors of the sky at sunset
with a touch of gold. This trout I give
to you and your children in your quest
with rod and line. And when you catch one
he will remind you of Me
and of the great love
I bear mankind."

Late afternoon on a solitary pond.

Random Casts

A Preface

I am a born traditionalist. I have a passionate love affair with bamboo rods, canvas waders, leather brogues, willow creels, and Quill Gordons. I suspect I am a product of an earlier period that embraced simpler times. Old school, perhaps, but secretly I rather enjoy it. Maybe I am just old enough to say that I have been there, and age does have its privileges. Now I may choose to fish any way that I care to: upstream with a dry fly, downstream with a wet, or just swinging a big bucktail across a large pool.

I humbly beg forgiveness from those who choose more modern tackle and weighted techniques in their pursuit of trout. Before being hooked and played, however, allow me to make a full admission of not being totally pure. I, too, have been guilty of sin. It required a considerable amount of thought and worthy sacrifices to the angling gods before switching from silk to nylon fly lines and synthetic leaders. Laziness was my only excuse, although I still maintain that a quality silk fly line casts admirably on a cane rod, and silkworm gut lies out as straight as the proverbial arrow.

With all due respect to the latter day fly tyers, and there are many good ones who can tie or sculpture a replica well enough to make a natural insect stand up and proclaim, "If I could only look like that!" (I suspect there may even be vanity among insects), I still prefer the older fly patterns. Tied in different sizes, they adequately suit my needs. Their poetic names soothe my spirit and inspire me to fish new waters in distant places. They appeal to me, more so than the latest attempts to dub every new fly with a Latin name that sounds cold and scholarly, possessing too much formality. Besides, I have never heard any two anglers pronounce these Latin names the same way. I fear that a former Latin teacher of mine would have been completely shattered (*amo, amas, amat…*).

Fifty years is a long time to cast a fly, or so it seems until you have crossed that river. My fondest wish would be for fifty more. Nevertheless, the first five decades have been priceless. I have been fortunate enough to have lived in an era that included fly tyers and cane rod-builders who were pioneers in their own rights. The hours spent alongside the fly tying vises of the Darbees, Fulsher, DeFeo, Herb Howard, and many others were not only memorable, but incredibly informative. The same affection is given to rod builders Jim Payne, Wes Jordan, and George Halstead for their kindness. They taught me to appreciate the "lovely reed."

With humility I have listened to Guy Jenkins, Sparse Grey Hackle, and Herman Christian add their special blends of color and touch to tales of Gordon, Hewitt, and LaBranche.

The Catskill Mountains are my home, and so are the rivers that flow through this bedrock of American fly fishing. The number of fishermen who remember many of the rivers now buried in the watery vaults beneath the reservoirs is rapidly dwindling. The Delaware River, so famous today for large brown and rainbow trout, was a warm water haven for all the six-inch bass you cared to hook in a day's fishing. And I vividly recall steam shovels atop the dam at the Pepacton Reservoir. Before this big lake was built, you could catch an ample supply of coarse fish all the way up to Margaretville.

Dams aside, there can be little doubt that the building of the watershed has enhanced trout fishing in these mountains. The cold, tailwater releases have revived the rivers immensely. Trout inhabit rivers as never before, and for those who prefer deep-water fishing in the reservoirs, there are fish in the ten to fifteen-pound class cruising the depths.

If you are a romantic like the writer and care to exercise your legs, you can still find native brook trout in the cold water pools nestled in the headwaters of mountain streams. Granted, these fish are small in size, but perhaps they are the last remnants of trout fishing as it was once upon a time.

The leaves of a fly book are comparable to pages of a history book. Each one is filled with dreams and choices. It is my wish that all of your selections prove successful. Perhaps someday, with good fortune, we may even meet ... on my side of the river.

CANNONSVILLE RES.

WALTON

WEST BRANCH DELAWARE RIVER

10

MARGAR

PEPACTON RES.

DOWNSVILLE

DEPOSIT

W. BRANCH DELAWARE

30

17

EAST BRANCH

E. BRANCH DELAWARE

17

ROSCOE

BEAVERKILL

RIVER

DEBRU

LIVINGSTON MANOR

WILLOWEM

HANCOCK

97

Ne

17

DELAWARE RIVER

HANKINS

PENNSYLVANIA

CALLICOON

LIBERTY

Map by Roger Menard

CATSKILL TROUT RIVERS

mford

Schoharie Res.

Prattsville

Roxbury

Lexington

23A

Hunter

Catskill

Schoharie Creek

42

214

32A

32

Big Indian

Shandaken

Phoenicia

Saugerties

28

Esopus Creek

Olivera

urnwood

Boiceville

28

Kingston

W. Branch Neversink River

E. Branch Neversink River

Ashokan Res.

laryville

87

Grahamsville

Rondout Res.

209

NEVERSINK RIVER

55

17   TO NYS THRUWAY

TO ALBANY

NEW YORK STATE THRUWAY

TO NYC

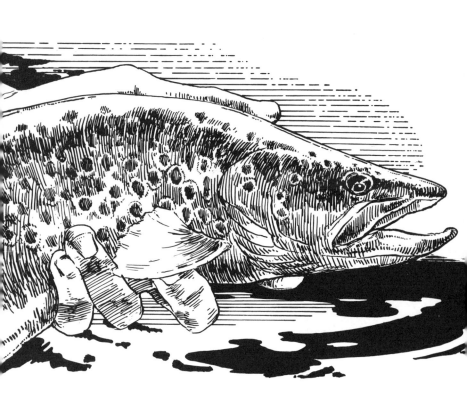

Mecca

An American angler visiting Great Britain or the Continent would be surprised to find that his free spirit would be largely curtailed. European trout streams, for the most part, are privately owned. It is a luxury to fish.

I once listened to a conversation among a Catskill fly shop owner and three British visitors, two gentlemen and a woman, who had just purchased non-resident licenses. One of the fellows spoke of his experiences on English rivers. He was delighted to have been accepted for membership in an exclusive club on a famous British river. His "beat" included a short stretch of water with several pools and certain restrictions. As he spoke, I shared in his enthusiasm, yet I could not help but feel how fortunate we are here in the States. I tried to imagine myself being limited to trout fishing half a dozen pools on one Catskill river for an entire season. The British visitors were thrilled to learn that for the price of a license they were entitled to fish anywhere on public waters. In the Catskills, this means enough quality water to fish so that the average angler need never revisit the same water twice in any given season.

Even a novice fisherman would have no problem in finding access to public waters. The State of New York has done a remarkable job in acquiring angler access to many of the Catskills' abundant trout streams, many of which have historical angling significance.

The veteran angler knows his favorite rivers intimately. By memory alone, he can tell you where every ledge, stone, pebble, and snag lies in any given pool. He probably can fish it blindfolded and catch trout (well, almost).

Because this book is about fishing Catskill waters and is for the enjoyment of the uninitiated as well as the experienced angler, I feel that it is appropriate to mention the classic rivers and include a brief description of each. There are a number of fishing maps available at tackle shops describing individual rivers.

There are eight major trout rivers in the Catskills: the Beaver Kill, Willowemoc, Esopus, Schoharie, East Branch of the Delaware, West Branch of the Delaware, Neversink, and the main Delaware River.

The Beaver Kill parallels Route 17 from the town of Roscoe in Sullivan County to its confluence with the East Branch of the Delaware River at the town of East Branch. There is public access parking on Old Route 17 following the river's course. Brown trout predominate. Above Roscoe to its source, the Beaver Kill has limited open water. Most of this section of river is privately posted.

The Willowemoc River in Sullivan County joins the Beaver Kill at Junction Pool in Roscoe. There is public access on Old Route 17 that also parallels the river. There are sections upriver that are accessible on town roads, but there is some posted water. Again, brown trout predominate, with wild brook trout found in the headwaters.

The Esopus Creek in Ulster County has open water from Big Indian to its confluence with the Ashokan Reservoir. There are designated access areas on Route 28 that follow the river's course. There are also pull-off areas (unmarked) on adjacent roads. Wild rainbow trout and brown trout are the main species of fish in this river.

The Schoharie, further to the north in Greene County, has public access on Route 23A from the town of Hunter to Prattsville before entering the Schoharie Reservoir. These were the home waters to Catskill fishing legend and fly tyer, Art Flick.

The Neversink River is steeped in angling history. It was on the Neversink (now partially under the reservoir of the same name) that Theodore Gordon, father of American fly fishing, lived, wrote, and tied flies. The river is formed by two branches, the East and the West, that join and flow into the Neversink Reservoir. Both sections of river are heavily posted. Below the reservoir, coldwater releases in the river offer the angler brown trout fishing. County roads follow the river and offer public access.

The East Branch of the Delaware rises in Delaware County north of Roxbury. There is good access from Route 28 in Arkville to the Pepacton Reservoir. Below Margaretville prior to entering the reservoir, the river is on New York City property. A watershed fishing permit is required. Brown trout are most common, with the occasional rainbow trout also being caught. Below the Pepacton Reservoir, coldwater releases enhance the brown trout habitat. There is access on Route 30 from the dam in Downsville to the East Branch's confluence with the Beaver Kill. From there, Route 17 follows the river to Hancock where it is

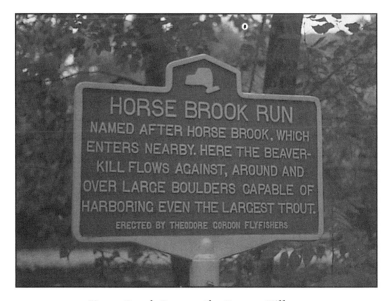

Horse Brook Run on the Beaver Kill.

joined by the West Branch of the Delaware to form the main
Delaware River.

The West Branch of the Delaware River originates near
Stamford and courses through farming country along Route
10 until it flows into the Cannonsville Reservoir. Below the

A Beaver Kill brown trout.

reservoir from the town of Deposit to Hancock (Route 17),
coldwater releases offer the angler good fly fishing.

The main Delaware River is big water. It has native
stocks of rainbow and brown trout. The entire river system
is open to the public (Route 97 parallels the river), but there
is limited access because of landowner posting. One may
wade or float the river in a boat via the boat launching
access sites. Guide services are available. It might be advisable for a newcomer to these waters to hire a guide and learn

the river. There are large trout in these big waters from Hancock to Callicoon.

The larger river systems mentioned offer only a portion of the opportunities available to the fly fisherman. There are a myriad of smaller streams and tributaries of the main rivers that support trout and offer less angling pressure.

Part of the joy of fly fishing is exploring new waters. In your travels you will surely meet fellow anglers willing to share trout lore and swap flies. Many long friendships have been born on the banks of a trout stream.

Back in the 1960s when Rocky Mountain and western trout fishing were really beginning to generate interest with eastern anglers, I happened to cross trails on the Beaver Kill with a western visitor. Naturally, I was curious as to why an angler with access to such superb trout fishing would choose to fish heavily pressured eastern waters. He told me that since boyhood he had read about the historic Catskill rivers. He had made a promise that someday he would visit these legendary waters.

And so to Mecca he came.

Opening Day

Opening day of the trout season is the rebirth of an angler's soul. The long, cold days of winter have retreated from the rays of a lengthening sun. The sap that poured from the ancient maples a month ago has ceased. Crocuses point their way to the skies through a shaded snow bank. Yesterday, I spotted two spring-spawning rainbows lying at the tail of a pool in a small stream flowing behind my home. These signs leave no doubt that the icy days of winter are numbered.

Fly tackle that lay dormant during hibernation has been retrieved from a closet, scrutinized for wear, and repaired. A fresh coat of varnish found its way on an old cane friend of mine, a two-year-old promise kept. A few, favorite wet flies were tied and have found a place in an old, worn, leather fly book.

Age, attitude, and experience all play their roles on this sacred date marked on the calendar and anticipated much like a child awaiting the last week of December. To the young angler, ready since the last day of the season past, this is the culmination of the highest form of cruelty that the state and its laws can inflict.

The young enthusiast, endowed with aggressiveness and a gymnastic ability, is obsessed with catching fish, as many as his cunning devices will allow. Brute force is the key to success, usually involving some sort of hardware or a wiggling, natural creature of the manure pile wearing a necklace of lead several inches above the hook. His plan is simple: *scorched earth!* Hit four rivers from top to bottom from the wee hours before dawn until the last light of day. If things are going well, he may even investigate another one or two hotspots on the way home. Frozen feet, leaky hip boots, and numbed fingers are badges of honor accepted by this young warrior. A bag of sandwiches made in haste the night before have been devoured and washed down with a thermos of cold coffee by 9:00 AM in the comfort of a heated automobile. Arriving home well after dark, he will make a few phone calls to angling friends, of course, advising them of his skill and stealth. But he must keep his cool and leave the impression that all of his good fortune—never luck, mind you—was done in a relatively short time. Oh yes, he got his limit!

The next angler is a self-appointed guru, well guided by scientific minds and angling journals. You know the sort. He's fully armed with every gadget known to anglerdom. (His latest is a midget mini-vac to remove dust from the spaces between rows of flies.) He is reassured by weather reports and well-kept diaries that conditions will be poor, if not downright impossible, for flies to be hatching on the first day of the season. In fact, according to his records, the last year of ideal conditions on opening day was in 1875. Besides, his guide to hatches advises him that the first trout will not rise until 1:25 PM on the third Tuesday of the month. Therefore, based upon all current data available, it is impractical to fish at all. It is much wiser to stay home and procrastinate. And this he does.

That evening, another fisher brave enough to follow his hunches informs the well-advised angler that the rivers were not that bad, water levels were within their banks, and a warm sun had a few naturals floating in the back eddy of a lovely little pool. Two wild brown trout were taken on a number sixteen Quill Gordon dry fly. There is dead silence on the phone!

Experience and time will temper an angler. After decades of floating a fly over a fish, angling takes on new meanings. Long gone is the lust for the wanton slaughter of fish. When a trout is dispatched, it is with the utmost respect and gratitude. The preparation of the feast is made with equal honor.

The river, now a cherished friend, has shared its secrets with one who cares to observe it through the glass window of water. Much beauty lies within the banks and the distant purple hills. Wildlife abounds in the adjacent fields and swamps. Deer trails and their crossings are familiar. So are the swallows that nest beneath the covered bridges, and the muskrat cruising the river with a jaw full of reeds.

Opening day to this angler is special, very special indeed. More often than not he will seek out the quiet places, not known for their quantity of fish, but for an abundance of memories. If he is luckier than most, he will share it with his wife, who has spent a lifetime as the perfect companion exploring trout waters near and far. A pleasant lunch and a cup of tea will accompany them to a high bank overlooking the river. They will reminisce of the Hendricksons that floated into the mouths of hungry trout and the difficult evenings of fussy fish feeding on Sulphers. "Remember when you caught that nineteen-inch brown trout one afternoon in May?" "Yes, and remember the time you lost that big fish beneath that tree over there?"

Lunch finished, they decide to make the first cast of a promising year. He follows his wife through two runs and a series of pools, fishing a pair of wet flies. Neither of them raises a fish. A red-winged blackbird balances itself on a streamside branch, announcing his arrival to the world. They return to their knoll for a cup of hot tea and salute their little friend. They take the old cane rods down and retreat from a cold north wind.

A new season has begun.

Choosing a fly on a northern pond.

First Impressions

Our first meeting was our last. I never knew his name, never heard of him afterwards, and never saw him again. Yet he left an indelible mark upon me. I still see his shadow silhouetted in my mind and in the eyes of similar youngsters bewildered in their angling beginnings.

In my youth, Saturdays were extra special. Schoolbooks were put on the shelf, fishing tackle assembled, and mountains of sandwiches were stashed in my fishing basket. At exactly 4:00 AM, Uncle Jim and my cousin (we called him Little Jim) would pick me up in a 1936 pale green, Lafayette automobile. This was to be a day spirited with discovery and adventure. We would explore small brooks and streams teeming with scores of leviathan trout: brooks, browns, and rainbows! Local gossip had buzzed with stories of huge fish, and fishermen swore that these tales were true.

Our first stop was a small, neighborhood bait shop. Uncle Jim was familiar with the owner, a bright, blue-eyed Swedish man who prided himself with having the best bait in the county. He even spoke kindly to his little friends when he gently extracted them from their bins. "Ya ... ya ... vat a buuuty dis von iss," he would say lovingly as he laid each plump specimen in the waxy container. "Dey vill ketch da bik vuns." With a friendly grin he sent us on our way. Even now, decades later, through a momentary association that may trigger it, I can still hear the running water flowing through his bait tanks and smell the damp sphagnum that permeated the spring pre-dawn air.

When we got back into the car, Uncle would ask for a vote and a show of hands. "Which stream shall we fish today, boys?" Little Jim and I tried to be democratic about this generous offer, but after a quick deliberation we would always reply, "You know the best spots to fish. You pick it." Uncle liked that, and besides, we were just tickled pink to be there. Uncle would then light his long-stemmed pipe, put the old floor shift into gear, and the three of us were on our way.

The stream was clear that day. A warm, early May sun filtered through the hemlocks and gray birches that bordered both sides of the river. We jointed and strung our old bamboo fly rods, swung the willow creels over our shoulders, and followed each other single file down a narrow path. When we reached the river, we split up. Little Jim made tracks to his favorite hole. Uncle and I continued down the trail for several hundred yards until we reached a large

pool. This was Uncle's favorite stretch of water. He would
step out three or four feet into the current and position himself alongside a huge boulder that formed a break in the
river's flow. Then he would place a little wiggler behind a
dime-sized Colorado Spinner and flip it upstream. He
allowed it to drift beneath the remnants of an old stone wall
on the far bank and held it there, just letting the blade turn
slowly in the current. Uncle would stand there for hours
slowly puffing his pipe, never moving more than a foot
either way. Small trout would dart out from beneath the
undercut bank and nip away at his bait. Because Uncle was
a patient man, he was usually rewarded for his efforts. Two
fish in his basket were plenty. He liked to have a pair of trout
for his Sunday breakfast.

My pool was dark and deep, nestled within the remnants of an old V-dam built many years ago. Trout loved to lie beneath the wet logs that protruded from the sides of the structure. I removed my basket, sat down with my legs crossed on the mossy bank, and tossed my bait into the flecks of foam in the swirling current. Then I sat and waited, always anticipating a pull from one of those *huge* trout. Surely they had to be in this pool!

Several hours passed with no strikes. I had begun to doze off, when I noticed a hesitation in the line. I waited for a few seconds and then pulled the rod with all my might. A small golden shiner flew through the air and landed on the moss behind me. I thought about keeping him just to let Uncle know that I had really caught a fish, but then changed my mind. I removed the hook from the shiner and dropped him with a small splash back into the pool.

I tossed my baited hook into the dark waters and then reached for a sandwich in my creel. I was halfway through lunch when I heard the cracking of a branch behind me. I turned and saw the image of a man emerging from the growth of the dark underbrush. He was tall, thin, and dressed in a pair of rumpled black pants with a faded, mismatched suit jacket. His white shirt was soiled, the collars turned up at the edges, and around his neck was a thin black tie. A worn felt hat encircled his head. Over his shoulders hung a large willow creel, and he wore calf-high rubber boots.

My old fly reel started to click, and I turned my head back towards the river. The rod was bent, the line vibrating excessively from the depths of the pool. I searched for the flash of a fish but saw nothing. The line was stationary. I was hung up. Try as I might, it would not budge. "Need any help, lad?" asked a quiet voice behind me. It was my visitor. He spoke with a strong Irish brogue, the corners of his mouth stained with brown tobacco juice. "Sure, mister!" I said. He waded in, grabbed my line, and pulled it free, but the frayed leader gave way about a foot up from the hook. Wading ashore and sitting down beside me, he assisted in putting together a new rig. The old gent showed me a few knots that I had never seen before and a new method of attaching my hook to a three-foot leader. Then he baited my hook. I flipped my new rig into the pool. "Thanks for your help, mister," I said as he rose to his feet. A smile wrinkled from his mouth as he turned towards the trail.

I couldn't help but notice his fine bamboo rod fitted out with a well-made reel. A beautifully tied dry fly hung from the fly holder above the grip. This was tackle I had often admired, but it was a choice that time or fate had not yet decided to cast my way. Eyeing his creel, I could not resist calling out to him before he moved out of sight. In a timid voice I asked him politely, "Did you have any luck today, mister?" He smiled, walked slowly back towards me, and opened the lid of his creel. Four brown trout, fourteen to seventeen inches long, lay in the green ferns, tails slightly bent. With eyes bulging and mouth open, I stood there speechless. He smiled again, closed the creel, and patted me on the head. "Good luck to you, my little friend. ... May they all be the biggest of trout."

The trip home was exciting. Uncle told us of his cunning patience and how he had caught his two trout for Sunday breakfast. Little Jim also caught two fish. I hooked and released one small fish, but could not stop talking about those brown trout lying in the depths of that large creel and the dry fly dangling from the old fisherman's rod.

That chance meeting between a seasoned, caring, fisherman and a young boy was the spark that ignited my lifelong love of fly fishing. The old fisherman lit the candle, and the flame still burns brightly.

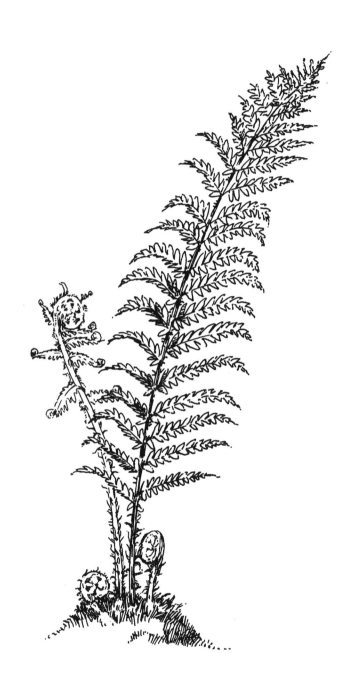

Small Streams

Far from the lush river in the fertile valley many miles below, wild brook trout dart from beneath undercut banks. The icy current yields meager pickings of drifting food. It is a lean life in the headwaters of small streams.

In this beautiful world of moss-covered rocks, miniature waterfalls, and banks laden with aged hemlocks, adult brook trout rarely surpass six or seven inches in length. On rare occasions, a plump nine-incher may take your fly. A twelve-inch brookie is a trophy.

In these shaded rivers the backs of the brook trout are dark olive with vermiculated markings. The fins, one of the more distinguishing characteristics, are orange and black, tipped with ivory. The sides have yellow spots with a sprinkling of smaller, bright red dots surrounded by pale blue halos. Dressed in annual fall spawning colors, the brook trout is the crown jewel of northern waters.

Unlike those in the big rivers, pools in small mountain streams are usually nameless, and I often take the liberty of naming them on my home waters. It pleases me and adds a touch of familiarity. First, there is Coyote Crossing, where in the dead of winter I have seen old bushy tail (the true gray ghost of the woods) pick his way across the tail of this ice-covered pool. Gray fur glistened in the sunlight when his final leap cleared a snow bank. In summertime this is good dry fly water.

And there is Fiddlehead Run. In the spring of the year, Ostrich Ferns push their way up in gnarled clumps through the rich soil above the high water mark. When steamed, these succulent greens are the perfect companion to the first, few, wild brook trout of the season. The trout should be cooked to perfection in an old, blackened cast iron pan, and a hearty libation is in order.

The Bearpaw is an old favorite. Black bears seem to enjoy poking around this section of river. In late fall after the first snows cover the ground, bear tracks cross the river, sometimes singly and other times a sow with a set of smaller tracks in tow. Their destination always points to the high ridges, undoubtedly seeking the comfort of a winter bear hole. I once hooked a leviathan in this pool on a dry fly in late summer. He nipped my offering ever so gently, then went upstream with all the power he could muster, tearing line off my reel at breakneck speed. He made an about-face and shot back into the pool beneath the safety of an undercut bank. The trout bored in and finally laced my leader neatly among the roots of a huge hemlock. I waded in as far as I could to gather up the remains of my leader. The white wings of a Coachman fly lay visible beneath the current, the hook firmly set in one of the roots. I would have liked to have seen that fish. The thought still haunts me.

Mink Pool is the deepest pool in the river. Whitewater rushes into the head of the run and then swirls into a deep green pool. The bottom is a mixture of gray cobblestone and rose-colored pebbles. As summers wane and autumns approach, I have counted thirty small brook trout lying motionless in this pool, hovering over a bed of red and yellow leaves. I discovered a mink's den not quite fifteen yards up the far bank of Mink Pool. I came upon it by accident one day while pausing to repair a leader tippet. When the first mink appeared, the shadows cast from the great hemlocks offered me adequate camouflage. Head erect, with piercing, beady eyes, the slender dark body probed every nook and cranny with surgical precision. The mink had not yet entered the water when a school of trout went into a frenzy, frantically circling the pool. With a quick side-glance, I noticed another mink sliding down a ledge at the head of the

Where the brook trout hide.

run. At water's edge, the undulating body moved swiftly but quietly among the craggy rocks. My attention shifted back to the tail of the pool. The first mink had a small brook trout in its tightly clenched jaws. With little hesitation he scurried up the bank with the prize, followed in quick pursuit by the second mink. They both disappeared into a small crevice. In a matter of moments, all was quiet. The school of brook trout lay motionless in the bottom of the pool. Colored leaves fluttered down from the treetops amidst a cool, fall breeze.

Fly fishing for brook trout on the headwaters is pure and simple. There are no frills, nor need for an abundance of burdensome tackle. Stalk and stealth will hook more trout than all of the fly books an angler could possibly carry. While larger rivers may accommodate many rods, these smaller waters are not favorable for a social gathering. They are best fished alone. This is intimate fishing.

The choice of tackle is uncomplicated. A small rod in the six to seven-foot length is fine. The short rod on a small stream will allow for fewer branch and leaf hookups. Most casts are short, delivered by either overhead or side-cast methods. I use several small cane rods with lines that execute well on short casts. Leader length should be kept to a minimum, especially if there are fast riffles. A shorter leader can be controlled a lot easier on fast water floats. The plan is to cast directly and precisely with less time spent retrieving excess line. A seven-foot leader is my first choice, but I will go to a nine-foot leader if water conditions warrant it. The tippet size depends on the size of the fly. A small selection of flies is more than enough for these headwaters. I also use a small, finely meshed wooden net. Old timers used to carry a combination net and wading staff along the river. It is still a good idea.

Fishing a dry fly on rapid waters.

Early season successes on little rivers depend largely on water temperature and water levels. Patches of snow often remain hidden well into the month of April, when snowflakes can still obscure a steel-gray sun. Winter is reluctant to retreat. The headwaters are high, thin, and clear. Brook trout lie on the bottom of deep holding pools. Their metabolism is low and they are hesitant to move any distance to chase a fly. For the fisherman, this can be a difficult time. There are no quick remedies or silver bullets in early season fly fishing.

Take note, also, of these early season trout. The underside will show a blackish tint, evidence that these fish are holding bottom. In the summer months, when they are closer to the surface, the belly will become increasingly lighter until the pearl-ivory color is evident.

Stonefly, Caddis, or Mayfly nymph imitations and big wet flies, either single or in pairs, are effective. Some reliable patterns include the Gold-ribbed Hare's Ear, March Brown, Quill Gordon, Black Gnat, and the Leadwing Coachman. Brighter patterns that I still like to use, especially for brook trout, include the Parmachenee Belle, Queen O' Waters, Montreal, and perhaps a Wickham's Fancy. These brighter patterns can be wonderful dropper flies.

It takes a lot of effort for a trout to kill and swallow a baitfish. Perhaps this is why the strike is so violent on a streamer fly. You can feel the hit solidly as the vibrations travel up the rod and through your shoulder. This is even more pronounced when the fly is taken on the downstream swing. High water allows the fly to move unobstructed at an even speed. Low water can create problems when exposed boulders interrupt the path of the fly. In low water, it is probably a better plan to cast up and across the stream, allowing the fly to sink where it can be worked slowly in the deeper pools.

Any of the traditional streamer flies and bucktails can be productive choices. My preference lies with the Gray Ghost,

Brown and White Bucktail, and, of course, the Muddler Minnow. For a little color, the Dark or Light Edson Tigers and the Mickey Finn are fine. Sizes eight and ten are my favorites. As spring progresses, anticipation stretches into reality; trout lose their sluggishness and become more receptive to the fly. You may be working your way downstream fishing wet, picking up the occasional trout, when you happen to notice a fish, the first of the season, surface feeding in a small back eddy. They are up to the dry fly!

On my little river, the swallowtail butterflies drifting up and down the valley indicate that dry fly fishing has started. Trout will disperse and move into the runs and fast pocket water, but never too far from the sanctuary of cover. This is a magic time for the fisherman who likes to fish the floating fly.

The headwater streams do not have the large hatches witnessed on the big waters. There may be sporadic early season hatches of Quill Gordons and a few Hendricksons, but only a smattering. Caddis hatches might be a little more concentrated, but the hatches are not numerous, nor do they last for any length of time. For this reason, the need for exact imitation is not as important as it would be on a larger river. More important are good floating flies with stiff hackle and quality hair to cover the fast pockets and riffles. I like the hair wing flies, traditional patterns, and a few dressings of my own. Calf tail, either natural or dyed, is very effective when tied in for the wings of many patterns. In fact, I usually substitute hair for a pattern that calls for a quill wing. Size is important. Dry flies in sizes fourteen through eighteen will suffice. I would be very cautious about using excessive hackle on dry flies. If it is too bushy, or if the hackle is too far back on the hook, it will act as a weed guard and will result in missed strikes. Years ago, having been plagued with missing fish in fast water, I decided to try a little experiment with hackle. I tied the equivalent of a size fifteen hackle on a number fourteen hook, giving me more

A small stream trophy brook trout.

gape and eliminating most of the weed guard effect. The percentage of fish hooked was much higher.

If I had to choose one fly to fish the fast water it would be the Hair Wing Royal Coachman in various sizes. Despite the fact that it departs from the exact imitation theory, its fish-attracting qualities are truly remarkable.

The large rivers suffer from the broiling heat of July and August, their sun-baked pools limiting the fishing to morning and evening. The shaded headwaters, however, continue to offer good, dry fly fishing and can be fished successfully throughout the day. Sparse Caddis fly hatches, and terrestrials, combined with cold water temperatures, keep the native brook trout active even at noon. But this is when stealth becomes important. Low water makes them wary. It is great fun to watch them dart from an undercut bank and chase a drifting fly. At the same time, if you are careless with your casting and wading, the telltale wake will also move from the tail of a pool swiftly towards the deeper water, and the fish are gone for the day.

If you are careful, you will often spot fish lying at the lip of the pool. These fish can be extremely difficult to take. Not only does the light splash of a fly line frighten them, the motion of the line while false casting can distract them as well. I have seen trout head for cover while the line was falling and had not yet touched the surface of the water. On the other hand, if the cast is successful, it can be exciting to watch a trout in full view drift back with open mouth and take a fly.

In September, with the leaves beginning to turn and the fall season approaching, nature becomes busy. Deer are beginning to wax fat on wind-felled apples. Bears, having reaped the blueberry harvest, are searching for an early mast crop necessary for that long winter's nap. Brook trout begin to move up the main river and tributaries to spawning sites. The colors of the fish are breathtaking. Amidst the beauty of the trout and the river, a sort of melancholy sets over an angler. Although a few weeks of fishing remain, he realizes that another season is coming to an end.

One late October, well after the season had ended, I went for a walk and came upon a low-water pool. The bottom was flecked with silhouettes of small brook trout. From the riffles below, four more brook trout moved up into the tail of the pool. They disappeared among the shadows.

Shadblow ... Can the Quill Gordons be far behind?

Quill Gordons and Hendricksons

Intermittent snowflakes blew hard on the heels of an icy north wind. The East Branch was cold and running high. Traces of white snow lay hidden behind a wet, decaying log. Above the water's edge beside an old deer trail, the bleached bones and weathered hair were all that remained of a fallen whitetail. It was well after midday in late April when I chose to seek shelter amidst a grove of young red pines. My perch was on a high bank with a view of a large pool directly below me. Several small stoneflies circled my arm, searching and probing before settling on my sleeve. With folded wings they crawled about aimlessly, seeking refuge in the creases of my shirt. I raised my arm and blew gently. They fluttered away, disappearing into a thicket of leafless willows.

The angle of an uncertain sun had shifted, removing silver streaks of glare from the river. Damn, it was cold! I pulled the collar of my wool shirt further up my neck. I was about to clean my eyeglasses when I caught the glimpse of a faint rise beneath an overhanging bush inches from the far bank. Ten yards further downstream another circle appeared, then another. I slipped down to the river's edge for a closer look. Little mayflies, with dun-colored wings erect, were floating past me. At first I had to search for them, but gradually they began to appear in greater numbers, several of them at rest, swirling about in a small back eddy. The rising trout across the river began feeding more earnestly, drifting from side to side, sipping in the unaware duns at will.

Gusts of winds sweeping upriver blew little cat's paws across the pool as I fumbled through my fly box with half-numbed fingers. I chose a small, number sixteen Quill Gordon. When the final knot was pulled tight on a 4x tippet, I waded into position, eyeing the downstream-feeding fish. Another heavy gust of wind shot over the treetops and put my fly four feet short of the mark. On my second try, the cast lay perfectly. The fly floated without drag into the open mouth of a feeding trout. Within seconds the fish was downriver, doggedly hugging the far bank. I kept light tension on the trout, just enough to keep him from entering the tangled undergrowth. He began to tire, slowly drifting towards the middle of the river, and I carefully worked him into the slack water near the bank behind me. After a few moments the fish, gills pulsating, lay in the depths of my net. I released all seventeen inches of him.

Gazing upriver, I could see other trout feeding, apparently unaffected by my tussle with the first fish. By now the duns were pouring down the river. Smaller trout were in the shallows, gorging themselves on the struggling insects. I doused my Quill Gordon with fly-dope, then waded upstream, false casting my way into position. The final throw landed the fly just above the fish. As it drifted to the side of a large boulder, a trout swirled, inhaling the fly. There was a pause, then a spray of water followed by a heavy surge. The fish bored deep, then shot downstream, my fly line trailing in the cold, dark water. This trout knew his domain well. He made an about face, working his way slowly upriver, seeking sanctuary among the roots near the far bank. I felt a dull vibration as the leader entwined itself among the watery tangle. I lightened up on the tension, but my luck came up short. This trout had found his freedom.

Within the next two hours I raised a dozen fish, releasing nine of those hooked. They were all brown trout, wild, with good color, averaging between nine and twelve inches.

By now the hatch began to dwindle, fading into this day's history. I resumed my place on the bank and lit my pipe. It was a good afternoon, an early-season day one looks forward to after a long winter of dreaming.

Quill Gordons herald in the dry fly fisher's season. It is the first major hatch that will pull trout from the depths of the pools and put them on a surface-feeding spree. Given the early season conditions of high and roily waters, it is remarkable that these delicate little mayflies survive in their mysterious world. They are very resilient insects.

Although anglers can expect to see them by the third week in April, the Gordons may appear a week or so earlier, or later, depending on temperatures and water levels. If conditions are ideal, dry fly fishing can be superb. If this be the case, I would strongly suggest an angler place himself in the thick of it as often as possible. The reason for this is that weather patterns at this time of year are so unpredictable. Should severe rains raise and cloud water levels, it could be the demise of this hatch for several days or even for the remainder of the season. Late April and early May are unsettling times on the river.

After the Quill Gordons have peaked, yellow forsythia and green pussy willows signal the emergence of the Hendricksons.

It was early afternoon and, although chilly, warm zephyrs floated up and down the river. Fifty yards downstream, the river made a slight dogleg turn, becoming narrower and deeper. Several fallen trees lined the far banks with protruding limbs leaning well beyond the edge. The water was gin clear, but running a little high. I could see trout feeding in the run below the turn where a small brook entered the main stream. These were not subtle rises, but showy slashes with bubbles trailing in the current. With care, I moved downriver, staying back from the main trail so as not to disturb the rising trout.

Larger mayflies with dark slate wings made their appearance, some drifting by with wings erect, others struggling to lift their fragile bodies from the surface of the water. Trout, ever opportunistic, lay in favored feeding positions devouring the succulent morsels with little shyness. If the Gordons will entice fish to chase a fly, the Hendricksons trigger the larger trout into a feeding frenzy. The season is young and the sheer numbers and size of these mayflies cause fish to throw caution to the winds, making them vulnerable to a good presentation. Fortunate is the angler to witness this hatch at its peak on some large pool where he is alone with rising trout a river cluttered with floating mayflies.

I reached into my pocket and chose a number twelve Hendrickson dry fly with a heavy claret-pinkish cast to the body. I tested the knot and waded into position, concentrat-

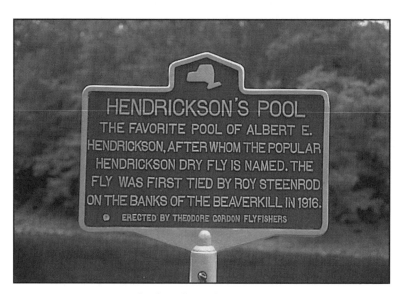

Hendrickson's Pool on the Beaver Kill.

ing on the "bank" fish in the tail of the run. The second cast floated down the lane and drew a response. My rod bent and the trout raced downstream, following with a series of short jumps. He then hovered in the middle of the run, boring deeper in the swifter current. I managed to coerce him with a slight sideways raise of the rod. He moved slowly towards my side of the river. The trout made a few small runs and finally came to rest in the slack water behind me. I slipped the net beneath the fish and raised him from the river. He measured fifteen inches. I released him, and with a swag of the tail he disappeared into the depths. While drying the fly, I remembered an incident that occurred in this same stretch of water several years ago on a day similar to this one. My wife, Lisa, and I were joined by Ron Hall, an angling companion and friend of ours, to fish the Hendrickson hatch. The previous two days of fishing had been very good. The weather was cooperative and the duns came off en masse.

Lisa was given first choice of water to fish. She elected to move further downriver to one of her favorite pools. Ron went straight out, and I moved upstream. It wasn't long before the first flies began to appear. Before I had even stepped into the river, Ron's rod was arced. I could hear his reel screaming as the fish raced through the pool. By the time I settled into my position, he was netting a large trout.

Hendricksons poured down the river in numbers we had not seen in years. It was prolific. Trout were rising all over—where we expected them to be, and in places where we would never cast a fly.

I had taken several small trout and managed to hook a few better fish. For two and a half hours we caught fish, changed flies, and caught more fish. At 4:30, as the hatch began to dwindle, fewer fish showed themselves and only a few insects rode the surface. Satisfied, I left my stretch of water and meandered downstream. Ron had also quit fishing. He was sitting on the bank gazing across the river, mesmerized by the day's events. I sat down beside him and we

Lisa choosing a dry fly.

talked about the extraordinary fishing. He produced one brown that he had kept, nineteen inches long and heavy in girth. He admired my eighteen-incher, another beautiful brown trout with exceptional color.

Then we centered on Lisa, who was coming up the old trail with a big smile. After a highly animated tale of doing battle with fish during the afternoon hatch, she asked me to reach into the back pocket of her vest. Somehow I knew what was coming. Yes, it was a fish—a brown trout, twenty-one and a half inches long.

Over the next several weeks the March Browns, Gray Foxes, Shad Flies, Green Drakes, and a host of other flies will make their entrances and exits over bright waters. Then, summer will blanket the mountains with heat and humidity, choking the rivers and shrinking them down to their barest bones, limiting fishing to early morning and dusk.

On a sultry August evening, waiting for a fish, any fish, to make an appearance in the fading light, my thoughts invariably return to the high, cold waters of April. I revisit spring, when snow patches line the banks of the river and the first Quill Gordons appear. It won't be long, only eight months to go. With fanfare, they will once again launch the angler into a sublime beginning.

Hatfish on the Esopus

The Esopus Creek is born high in the Catskills not far from her sister rivers, the Beaver Kill and the Neversink. Rising from cold mountain springs, the river begins its wandering descent down an ancient wooded valley, grinding and cutting a path that guides its waters to the distant Ashokan Reservoir. Below the Winisook the river quickens its pace, tumbling over hemlock-covered pools and flat cobblestone riffles. Small rivulets begin to filter into the main stream, widening the flow as it passes through Oliverea and Big Indian. These headwaters are the nurseries of young, fingerling trout—some wild browns, but mostly parr-marked rainbows spawned in a previous spring by a migration of rainbows from the expansive reservoir further downstream.

At Shandaken, more tributaries enter the main river, widening the channel. At Allaben, the river reaches its full crescendo as a discharge of cold water, part of a unique aqueduct system created by the city of New York in the early 1900s. The coldwater release enters the river via a tunnel known locally as the "portal." Eighteen miles north of the portal, water is stored in the Schoharie Reservoir, where it is then pumped beneath Balsam Mountain via the tunnel. The cold water is a blessing for the big river, especially during the heat of the summer, although at times, turbidity can be a problem for the fly angler. This annoyance can be heightened even further because the entire Esopus Creek and its tributaries are heavily endowed with red clay banks. After severe rainstorms, the entire river system becomes a nightmare of devastating effect that can last days, weeks, and even months. Several hurricanes in the mid-century literally tore the river to pieces. Gravel shifted, destroying pools and relocating streambeds. At several "bend" locations, railroad tracks adjacent to the river were twisted like pretzels. And this does not take into account the precious loss of fish life and insect populations. But in spite of nature and man-made ravages, the river still maintains a healthy wild rainbow trout population.

The river pushes past the old fishing village of Phoenicia, which for generations of Esopus anglers was Mecca. There are still remnants of old hotels and boarding houses where waders, willow creels, and brogues once hung from front porches. Sadly gone, however, are the smiling faces of Herman and Dick Folkert, owners of the old fishing tackle store on Main Street. For years their fine imported tackle served the needs of visiting anglers. Another landmark that disappeared was Elmer's Diner, a familiar meeting place for rainbow-seeking fishermen. All that remains is the shell of the diner nestled among overgrown bushes on old Rt. 28 just outside of town.

From Mount Tremper to Boiceville there are a series of long deep runs and white pocket water. Many of the runs are strewn with huge boulders and algae-covered rocks that make wading difficult.

At the Five Arch Bridge in Boiceville, the Esopus begins its final leg of a long journey that began in the distant, blue mountains. The river turns abruptly at the Bend Pool, races beneath the old railroad trestle, and finally comes to rest at the last pool, the Chimney Hole.

The entire river system has a good trout population. Wild rainbow trout are self-sustaining. The state, in an effort to further compensate anglers, plants thousands of brown trout into the river annually on a "put and take" basis. In the 1970s the state conducted a project with special fishing regulations to evaluate the brown trout population from the Five Arch Bridge to the Ashokan Reservoir. Final evidence was inconclusive and public support was questionable. With the exception of the Delaware River system and a few other rivers in the northeast, the Esopus, despite its problems, both natural and political, remains a fisheries manager's gold mine. It supports natural reproduction. The size of the rainbows on the entire river system ranges between six to twelve inches, with the occasional larger brown trout or hold-over rainbow spawners that remain in the river for whatever reason. The river also boasts a fall run of brown and rainbow trout migrating upstream from the Ashokan Reservior.

Although early-season big fish are taken occasionally on artificials, most are taken with various baits. Years ago, during the first few weeks of the season, pools were fished much harder than they are today. Cars were parked the full length of the river as fishermen encircled their favorite pools seeking spawning rainbows. There were always a few large spawners lying on the counters in local tackle shops, with word spreading in diners and hotels that big fish were being caught in the main stream. Good size fish were also taken in the tributaries, particularly the Chichester Creek and the Woodland Valley Stream.

I have never witnessed very good fly fishing on the main stream until the middle of May, save mild years when Quill Gordons come off in late April. Once, however, I can recall a sunny day on a big pool below Phoenicia when, for one hour in the early afternoon, winged black ants swarmed over the river in droves. Small rainbows appeared everywhere, gorging themselves. I caught a half dozen fish on a small ant pattern. Then, as quickly as the hatch started, it ended, and the trout vanished into the icy pools. Although I have looked for a repeat performance year after year, I never saw this hatch again.

The one characteristic that is consistent on this river is that when feeding in a large pool, several rainbows will begin rising simultaneously, gorging themselves for a short while, and then stop. In a period of time, maybe ten to fifteen minutes, they will begin to feed again. They are a moody fish, extremely fast strikers, and can be as fussy over fly patterns as well as any brown trout.

Esopus flies include all of the Catskill patterns tied in various sizes. The Quill Gordon, Hendrickson, Red Quill, Dun Variant, March Brown, Gray Fox Variant, Blue Winged Olive, and Red Fox, are all good dry fly patterns. The Hair Wing Coachman and the Adams are invaluable, fished in both fast water and pockets. Small Caddis patterns in tan and gray are also good floaters.

Wet flies have always been favorites on this river, maybe even more so than on other Catskill waters, because of the predominance of turbulent water. A reliable selection of wet flies includes the Gold Ribbed Hare's Ear, Leadwing Coachman, Blue Quill, and the Quill Gordon. After the middle of May, I would not be without the Wickham's Fancy, Campbell's Fancy, or the Greenwell's Glory as a dropper fly, and a small black-hackled wet as the tail fly. The wet flies should be tied sparsely in sizes fourteen through eighteen. There are also some good nymph patterns, particularly in shades of gray and olive. An all-black nymph in sizes twelve to eighteen is indispensable throughout the entire season.

The late Ray Smith, perhaps the valley's most well known fly tyer, tied up a three wet-fly rig that was extremely effective on the Esopus. The typical rig would include a Leadwing Coachman, a Gold Ribbed Hare's Ear, and his Wild Turkey pattern. Sometimes his rigs included the Orange Fish Hawk, Royal Coachman, and a Dark Cahill. He used many combinations. Incidentally, Ray lacquered the tips of the wings of his wet flies, both quill and feather, for uniformity and streamlined appearance.

Once in a while, I come across an old-timer wading the river, casting his three wet flies down a fast water riffle. Conversations always begin with Ray Smith. His team of three wet flies still performs magic on the river.

During the height of the fly season, angling pressure increases, particularly on the weekends. In order to avoid this, a local fisherman can pick his time, which means fishing during the week. Although intimate with the river for many years, it was not until the spring of 1970 that I experienced what was to be the beginning of my halcyon days on the Esopus. It lasted for seven glorious seasons. Here is how it all began.

Memorial Day is one of the busiest weekends on the river. In order to avoid angler congestion, I took advantage of the lighter traffic several days before the holiday began. Fly rod in hand, I walked the bed of the railroad tracks below Boiceville, planning to fish the Trestle Pool. Upon my arrival two fishermen were casting long fly lines over the entire pool. Having no inclination to join them, I crossed the old trestle bridge and continued on the path that led to the Chimney Hole. When I cleared the woods my plans were once again interrupted. A lone angler was standing at the head of the pool casting wet flies in traditional style, down and across, allowing the flies to swim in the fast current. I could have fished the tail of the huge pool, but declined, with no other reason except that I preferred to be alone.

Below the Chimney Hole, the river is deep with a moderate current. In places, there are large submerged boulders. At that time, this section of river was a no man's land to a fly angler, seen only by an occasional wandering, bait fisherman, or at night by a few local, walleye fishermen. The old iron chimney, which still stands today, sits on a high bank towering above the tail of the Chimney Hole. Directly across the river is a huge ledge overlooking a very deep pool. Below the ledge is a series of gravel runs and drop-offs. Wading here among the algae-covered boulders is difficult and hazardous, particularly when the river is high.

From my high vantage point I had a commanding view several hundred yards downriver. A glance upriver revealed the fly fisher's line still in the air. His casual fishing style suggested that he was camped out for the duration.

Gazing across the pool, I saw several swallows swooping down from the sky, skimming the surface. At first it was occasional, but within a half-hour's time the number of birds increased. Directly below the ledge pool at the head of the gravel run, I saw a fish swirl. Moments later a nose pierced the water's film. Several March Browns began fluttering on the surface. They were large and clumsy with mottled wings and yellow butter-like bodies. As the hatch intensified, numbers of these large flies attempting to dry their wings were carried downstream into the mouths of rising fish.

I pulled my fly book from my vest and put on a big number ten March Brown dry fly. It was a tie of my own that had grizzly and brown hackles with the same fibers for tails. The wing was Wood Duck, with a body of grayish-yellow dubbed fur. With a quick tug I tested my tippet for strength and eased my way into the water. As I began to feel my way out through gravel, mud, and boulders, I probed the bottom with one foot before letting the other fall. I had to lift my vest above my waders several times in order to avoid a soaking. Finally, I reached the gravel bar where I could wade and cast with relative comfort.

The fish continued to feed. Adding to the excitement, Caddis flies began to appear, breaking the water's film with desperate attempts to flee as the flash of fish swirled from beneath the surface. I resigned myself to the fish further downstream. I waded into position, lengthened my line, and made the cast. The fly landed six feet above the trout and floated down the feeding lane.

It was a slow, deliberate take, followed by a heavy pull. An explosion followed, spraying water in all directions. The white fly line knifed through the water as the fish went into high gear, hell-bent for the reservoir. The fish made a U-turn, moved upriver and sulked. I reeled as fast as I could, gathering in backing as quickly as my hand could turn the handle. Although seasoned in this sort of thing, my heart was in my throat. It was that split-second loss of contact that caused me to reel in even faster. When I felt the tension, I was relieved. The trout turned and headed downriver with a vengeance. The fly line and backing tore through the guides. The reel wailed. Turning full circle, he sped back upstream. I reeled, feeling him all the way. The fish began to edge towards the far bank, seeking the slack water to gather strength. I gave him more backbone on the rod and cau-

Anglers' access on the Esopus Creek.

tiously waded downstream onto the gravel bar. He had me perched on the edge of the deep water when he finally turned upriver, facing me. The current began to tax his resistance and I could see the silver body, a dark red stripe adorning his side. By working him to my side of the current, the fish turned sideways and surfaced. I coaxed him into a quiet piece of water near the bar and reached for my net.

The fly was solidly hooked in the corner of his mouth. I slipped the net beneath him and lifted. The big rainbow was safe in the mesh. I waded ashore, measured and weighed him—twenty-three inches, four pounds. Bright silver scales hung from the net. I dispatched him quickly, then rested on the bank, lit my pipe, and admired my prize. Although more than a quarter of a century has passed, the image of that brightly-colored rainbow lying on the grass bank surrounded by lavender and white phlox remains as vivid as the day I caught him.

After a short breather, I looked at the pool again. Thirty feet above where I had taken the first fish, another March Brown disappeared. I put on a new fly and picked my way out to the gravel bar. The fish had positioned himself perfectly. Two currents converged, floating every March Brown into his field of vision. Like his predecessor, this trout rose quietly but deliberately. The fly disappeared followed by a strong pull—another heavy fish on. He turned sharply, and within seconds was past me with three jumps downriver. The tug-of-war began with the head-shaking. Take a little, give a little, until, in the quiet shallow water, the spent fish lay in my net. I waded back to shore and placed the two fish side by side. This fish was twenty-two inches long and weighed three and a half pounds.

By now the hatch was subsiding with only a few stragglers coming off. I noticed two more trout feeding, but feeling content, I decided to clean my two fish and call it a day.

I knelt down in a small back eddy, drew my knife, and began to clean the fish. I heard a voice behind me. "They are two fine rainbows. I enjoyed watching you play them." I turned and recognized him as the angler I had seen fishing earlier at the Chimney Hole. He was a likeable chap named Martin Warnes, a local fisherman who tied his own flies. His easy manner and worn tackle suggested that he had taken his share of trout. We sat until dark, exchanging stories and swapping flies. The conversation continued on the trail, now lit only by the beams from our flashlights. We agreed to meet again during the following week.

Our rendezvous was a repeat performance of the first night we had met. Both of us were into fish, all rainbows, from sixteen to twenty-one inches. Marty killed one fish, and we released the rest. For the next three and a half weeks the fishing was superb.

As time passed and our successes continued, we agreed to save all the flies that caught fish over fifteen inches. The flies were put in our hatbands; hence, our term "hatfish" was born on the Esopus. After the third year, we ran out of space on our hatbands and transferred the flies to wooden picture frames. At the end of our seventh year, each frame was rimmed with well over one hundred and fifty flies.

As exciting as this exceptional fishing was, it only lasted for the month of June. After that, the big rainbows were gone, back to the depths of the reservoir. We were fortunate during our reign on the river because of the lack of competition. Most fly fisherman did not venture that far downriver, and bass season opened in the middle of the month, claiming many devotees.

Although we took additional trout in the ensuing years, the fishing slowly tapered off. Perhaps it was a cycle, or maybe it was the return of larger walleyes that invaded the lower water. I do know from reports and firsthand observation that six to eight-inch trout were found in the stomachs of Walleyes. Explanations are many, and all are speculative. I am sure fisheries' biologists could have narrowed it down, but, whatever the reason, the halcyon days for us had ended.

The only testament that remains today is a faded, weather-beaten carving in a tree along the trail to the Chimney Hole, just above the railroad trestle. On that tree is the name Martin Warnes and the date, 5/3/73. It is a reminder of the kind of fishing that passes through an angler's world, if he's fortunate, once in a lifetime.

A wild brown trout, small in size but big in spirit.

Cane

The end of World War II changed America forever. In many ways, it also ended a chapter in angling history. Prior to the war, save trolling, the casting angler had a choice of either a fly rod or a bait-casting rod. A bamboo fly rod, seven to nine-and-a-half feet in length, fitted with a single action reel and a gut leader attached to a silk fly line, were standard fly tackle. And it was not uncommon to see fisherman using automatic fly reels that were mounted either horizontally or vertically to the reel seat. Tied to the end of the gut leader was a fly, either single or in multiples. In the post-war period, even the venerable snelled fly lost favor.

Cane or metal bait-casting rods four-and-a-half to six feet in length were also popular. Casting reels were level-wind or free-spool. Even with anti-backlash devices, these ornate jewels had to be thumbed to prevent backlashes. Proficiency with these reels required many hours of practice and properly balanced tackle. Many fishermen never could get the hang of it. In the hands of a master, however, it was a beautiful sight to behold. Light silk casting lines could place small wooden plugs right on target with amazing accuracy.

Spinning was to change all this. Before the war, although practiced in Europe, spin fishing was virtually unknown in the U.S. After the war ended, it was introduced to these shores. Everyone became a caster overnight. It would be a long time before casting rods would emerge from the closet once again.

Plastics and nylon would also have their impact on angling. Even though nylon had been developed and advertised in the sporting magazines of the late 1930s (Weber marketed nylon leader material called Vec, and Lyons and Coulson marketed Ariflex), it wasn't until the war's end that it was utilized. Nylon quickly began to replace gut leaders and silk lines.

The advent of synthetics and glass fibers introduced new rod materials. This also had a tremendous impact on the cane rod industry. Only a handful of the quality, higher-priced rods would survive. Today, half a century later, several companies are still building bamboo rods, but of greater importance is the renaissance in cane rod building. More and more fine custom rod makers are emerging and renewing an interest among fly anglers.

Many of us born before or during the Depression were influenced by bamboo rods. The scent of varnish when an old bamboo rod is removed from the rod tube is pure tonic. Like a genie, the ancient past rises from the bottle with promises of good fortune to follow. The history and romance of cane enhances the moment even further. Therein lies the quality in bamboo called "soul."

Spar varnish, with its soft patina finish, allows the beauty of the grain to be admired. Oxidized ferrules, fingered over the years, have faded to a smoke-gray in color but still maintain their magical "pop" when separated. The reel seat remains tight even though the locking nut may squeak up and down the barrel threads. The guides, slightly grooved, bear honorable scars of past campaigns, and although the sun has bleached color from the silk windings, it remains as pleasing to the eye as when the rod was first purchased, maybe more so.

As the fishing seasons came and went, an assortment of cane rods found their way into my possession and I had the opportunity to meet some excellent rod makers. George Halstead, Jim Payne, and Wes Jordan were among the best— gentlemen all, and very receptive to my desire to understand the cane rod. What was quite impressive to me was that,

A classic split-bamboo rod.

despite the individual pride in their own work and subsequent competition for sales, they had a deep respect for and appreciation of each other as craftsmen.

During the late 1950s, George Halstead, living in Brewster, New York, built a splendid small rod for me, excellent for dry fly fishing on small streams. Some years later, after George had passed away, I brought the rod to Jim Payne to repair a tip section that had separated. Jim inspected the rod and told me he'd call when it was ready. One month later I received a note from him notifying me that the work was completed. Jim had matched everything perfectly. I admired his work, after which we sat down and discussed rods and rod actions. When it was time to leave, I reached for my wallet. Jim put his hand on my shoulder and in his quiet way said, "No charge, Roger, and please, when you see Kay Halstead [George's wife] send her my best regards." I did.

On another occasion, I was returning from a Maine fishing trip and stopped at the Orvis Company in Manchester,

Vermont, to pick up some rod parts. Wes Jordan was alone at the company's casting pool trying out one of his rods. He offered me the rod, a sweet eight-and-a-half-footer, to cast. We chatted for a few minutes and I asked him if he cared to try one of my cane rods. "Sure," he said, "let me see it." I handed him my Halstead, which had no name or identification label on the rod. Wes looked at the ferrules and the sliding bands. He grinned, and with a wink said, "When you see George, tell him I said hello!" I did.

Bamboo, a once-living reed tempered by the weather, hand-split, and transformed into a work of art by its maker, offers an angler a remarkable fly rod. A rod that fits the hand with fine balance and instant response is one to cherish for a lifetime. Like a fine violin, it resonates with pure joy.

Because no two pieces of bamboo are the same, no two bamboo rods are alike. In fact, two rods from the same craftsman, identical in size, weight, and labeled as the same model, may have subtle differences in action. These differences can be more pronounced in standard production rods, but this does not mean that they are inferior casting rods. On the contrary, some of these rods have excellent action and are pleasing to cast. Much of this depends on the ability and requirements of the individual angler. Good rod tapers of quality construction increase balance in the rod. The rod feels light in the hand and makes for enjoyable casting.

When cane rods approach the eight-and-a-half-foot length or longer, the weight factor becomes critical. If it is too heavy, the rod becomes unwieldy, usually tip-heavy. This causes fatigue when casting. The only way you can be sure to discover this is to put a line on the rod. Your casting arm will make the decision for you rather quickly.

As the years go by, you may develop a curiosity about rod making and rod building. It might begin with a lifeless piece of disheveled bamboo lying in the corner of some attic, or perhaps on a table at a flea market. On inspection you put the joints together and give it a few wiggles. You say to yourself, "Hm ... this feels pretty good and maybe ... with a little work, I can resurrect you to your prior dignity." There are no markings on the rod that indicate its origin. It is safe to assume that this was a good production rod.

Chances are that someone replaced the guides on this foundling with bulky, cotton thread windings of a different color, and slapped a thick coat of varnish over the entire rod. The cork grip is soiled and chunks of cork are missing, undoubtedly a result of too many snelled bait hooks being forced into the grip. The ferrules are in good shape, sound and tight fitting. All sections of the cane are fairly straight, and the glue lines are intact with no cane separation. The downlocking reel seat is also in good condition. You decide that the project is worth the effort. Having tied thousands of flies over the years, there is no reason why you cannot

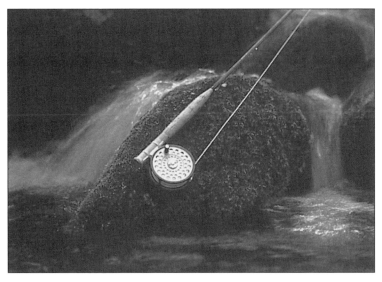

A miniature rod for intimate waters.

wind a guide on a rod. You have also had some experience in woodworking, and with a little homework, common sense, and patience, there is no reason why you can't bring this rod back to life. The tedious but rewarding work begins. If there is any possibility of the rod being vintage quality, it should be given to a competent rod maker for complete restoration.

Before you disassemble the rod, make a diagram of where the guides are or were on a large sheet of paper. On

Brookie on a Parmachenee Belle wet fly.

the older rods it may be easy to see the stain marks if the guide is missing. If you decide to add any extra guides (usually on the tip section), you will have to adjust the space between the guides.

First, the old guides must be stripped off the rod and the old varnish removed. A sharp knife or razor blade should take care of the windings. Be careful not to cut into the cane. Next, use a good varnish remover to dissolve the old finish. I would avoid scraping the finish off with a blade. There is a chance of shaving the precious outer cane too deeply. After the varnish has been removed on all sections, give it a rub-down with turpentine to remove all traces of the varnish remover and also to clean the rod.

If the reel seat needs replacing, this would be the time to do it. For our purposes, this reel seat is okay.

It is now time to replace the cork grip. If it just were soiled, with no evidence of heavy pitting, a good washing with soap and water, followed by a quick rinse with bleach and a final rinsing with water, should put the cork into new condition. In this case, the cork grip is in need of replacement. Until you are familiar with individual cork rings and with sanding them, it would be advisable to use a pre-formed grip, whatever style suits your needs. Using a knife, take the old grip off. With fine grade sandpaper remove any remnants of cork on the rod blank. Glue the new cork on with any of the rod epoxies available. As you are gluing, be sure to rotate the cork grip to a position that fits your hand comfortably. Avoid having any large pits positioned under your thumb or in any place that will rest on your fingers or palm. You can fill small pits in cork by mixing cork dust (saved from sanding) and color preserver to form a thick paste. Fill the holes, let dry, and carefully smooth the grip with fine sandpaper.

If there is a jiggle in the rod when you pretend to cast it, chances are there is a loose ferrule. If the ferrules are loose, remove them. In the process of removing the ferrule, it may be necessary to remove a pin. After locating the pin, take a fine punch and knock the pin out. Reset the ferrules with ferrule cement. It is not necessary to replace the pin. If the ferrules are nickel silver, and you wish to oxidize them (re-bluing), now is the time. There is a nickel silver oxidizing solution available on the market. Follow the directions on the package. If the ferrules are plated and will not accept bluing, just clean them up with a soft cloth and a little metal polish. Now you are ready to put the rod together.

Thread comes in either silk or nylon. The older rods were wrapped with silk, which makes a flatter and more attractive wind. Silk, however, is difficult to work with. It frays and soils easily. Nylon may be a little bulkier, but works well. With the thread type and color of your choosing, begin with the butt section. Start with the winding check, a small metal band at the front of the cork grip. The hook holder will be there. Wind the hook holder onto the rod. Decorative windings, if desired, are put just ahead of the hook holder.

Your choice of guides will be either the old-style bronzed or the newer stainless steel. I prefer the bronzed guides for aesthetic reasons. They enhance the older cane rods. Whatever style you choose, tape the new guides onto a piece of cardboard in the order they will be placed on your rod. Your first guide will be a stripping guide, often of carbide, but on the older rods, agate. Both types are readily available. File the feet of all your guides. A good taper will allow the thread to wind on more smoothly from the cane onto the guide foot. And don't make the new wrap too much longer than the original wrap. A narrow band is more pleasing to the eye. When all of the guides on all the sections have been completed and the tiptops have been replaced (with ferrule cement), you are ready to varnish the rod. Before you begin varnishing, run the wrapped windings very quickly through an alcohol lamp flame to remove excess fuzz and dust.

Some rod builders prefer to use color preserver on the windings before varnishing. I don't care to because it can cause the windings to crack or check with time. I prefer straight varnish, accepting a darker color on the winds.

No matter how well the rod has been wrapped, varnishing is the step on which the final product will be judged. Varnishing a rod at home is difficult at best. Dust and room temperatures are the most common enemies. Lacking special dipping tanks, an acceptable finish can be obtained using a good quality half-inch sable brush. Lately, I've tried some of the black foam, wedge-shaped brushes in the three-quarter-inch size, and have had very good results. The varnish should be fresh, high grade, oil-based Spar varnish. It must flow freely at room temperature. By applying light, thin coats with long, even strokes, you will eliminate drips and runs caused by a heavy buildup. It is very important to varnish in a room that has no traffic that can cause dust to circulate. When you finish a section, put it into a cabinet or some sort of container where it can hang undisturbed. It is of the utmost importance to allow that first coat to dry completely. Although the windings may appear to be dry on the surface, the interior might still be damp. I would let the rod dry for at least a week, more if humidity is high. In all, a total of four coats complete the rod.

Every time I have refinished one of these lovely pieces of cane, I cannot help but reflect on the history of the rod I have before me. What distant waters have yielded pleasant memories in the mind of some unknown angler? And how many trout has it led over the frame of a net? This I will never know, but as I lengthen fly line on familiar waters, a new chapter will be written on this once-forsaken child.

Some Thoughts on Feathers

An artist puts his impressions on canvas. A fly tyer puts his thoughts on a wire hook. Creating artificial stream-borne insects has always fascinated me. Like many anglers, I suppose, my younger days were spent searching for and scrounging up as many hand-me-down flies that I could get my hands on. Some of them were fair fish-takers, others (a good many on gut snells), were better off if they had been saved for posterity. Most sought after were the somber colored flies that were more effective for brown trout on my home waters. I would catch some browns on a few worn, gaudy patterns fished through a heavy rapid, but this was the exception rather than the rule. These early experiences left me with an open mind. You would be surprised at what a trout will swallow when he goes on a feeding spree.

Although my early fishing was often successful, I soon realized that most of my flies were much too big and lacked the necessary colors. Flies sold at the local hardware store were of no great help either. In many respects they were even worse than what I had in my fly book. Most of them were huge, bass-type flies tied on a number 2 or larger hook. The more I fished, the more I began to inspect insects both above and beneath the water. Autopsies on fish were also revealing. I could study the colors, sizes, and forms of insects they had fed upon.

It wasn't until I had the opportunity to visit WM. Mills and Sons on Park Place in New York City, that I had my first look at a real selection of trout flies. There were a myriad of them, all stored in bins beneath glass countertops framed by a wall of Leonard cane rods. Here was a whole new world at my disposal, and I resolved then and there to learn how to make my own flies. During the following winter I studied all the reading material that I could gather. There was, by no means, the volume of material a novice tyer has at his disposal today. For the most part, I was self-taught, learning the basic tying techniques through trial and error. My simple hand-tyed creations even caught some fish. It would be years later that I would sit down with some of the masters I sought out to perfect my fly tying.

It was very important to me in those early days to realize that I could use my own powers of observation and transfer them onto a hook. It is always best to tie flies using colors as *you* see them. Blend your hackles and dubbing material so that after a good soaking, the shades of color will be exactly what you want. Too often, many of the fly dictionaries will give the dressings in a loose fashion. Dun can come in a multitude of tones and it can be confusing, especially if you are imitating a particular insect with an exact shade. A lighter or darker color can make a fly a dismal failure when you see it on the water. There is not much room for error.

Fly tying and fly fishing have been practiced for centuries, but never in their long history has their following been as strong as in the past two decades. In these times of feathers aplenty, it would be hard for a novice tyer to comprehend the difficulties we experienced in collecting materials as recently as twenty or thirty years ago. The quality and quantity of necks alone in today's market would have fetched a small fortune in former days. Collecting run-of-the-mill feathers was easy enough, but acquiring first-rate feathers was another matter. Sources for gathering materials were limited and, for the most part, it required a considerable amount of individual ingenuity.

Tackle shops, although well stocked with rods, reels, and other angling paraphernalia, carried little in the way of fly tying materials. If they did have anything in stock, it was probably faded chenille and badly tarnished tinsel lying in a dusty drawer behind the counter. Materials were obtained through mail order catalogs, correspondence with fly tying friends, or hunters in the field. The better catalog companies, many of whom are no longer in business, were fairly reliable with their selection of materials. You must realize

Early season streamer flies.

that these vendors could not turn a profit with a warehouse full of merchandise returned by picky customers. Indeed, there was a considerable amount of finger crossing when your order arrived. Feathers, hair, and wing quills were of the greatest concern. Floss and tinsel were generally of good quality. In fact, some of the best French tinsel I ever used came from the old Herter's Company in Minnesota. You could buy the tinsel in bulk sizes. These large, heavy wooden spools felt like a small cannonball in your hand and performed the way tinsel was supposed to, adding flash and having enough weight to put a fly under the surface. I still have a little stash of French tinsel left on wooden spools for a few more flies.

Professional fly tyers were several steps ahead of the game. Major feather merchants would ship necks in bulk, usually fifty or a hundred to a box, in a single color with no return privileges. These bulk feather merchants were more interested in the millinery trade than they were in selling feathers to fly tyers. Ray Smith, a Catskill fly tyer of Esopus fame, had regular bulk shipments of necks arriving from New York. "Barnyard chickens," he would call them. Once in a while he would call ahead and let me know when the shipments would arrive. We would spend several afternoon hours sorting and grading necks. It offered me a rare opportunity to hand pick some choice necks.

Natural blue dun, a glut in today's market, was only a dream to fly makers in those years. If you were lucky enough to find some, chances were good that the color was wrong. It was either too light, too dark, stems too thick, or not even close to what you had in mind. If you found one that suited your fancy, the odds of duplicating it were next to impossible.

The only alternative to natural dun was dyed blue dun. Granted, they were not authentic, but contrary to popular belief, these feathers did have merit. You could match colors with regularity, and they caught trout. Most duns were dyed from cream necks, which were always plentiful. I always favored the red grizzly neck dyed in a bath of armor-gray Tintex. (As far as I know, this color is no longer available). The brown tips of these dyed feathers would be highlighted when you held them up to the light. It was about as close as you could get with an imitation.

Most roads for the quest of natural dun usually wound up at Harry Darbee's doorstep. In the early 1970s, while dining in their kitchen on blue dun eggs for breakfast, Elsie suggested that I take some eggs home and raise my own gamecocks. "Why not?" I said. And so the adventure began. The first thing I did was to give the eggs to a friend, a local farmer, who put them under one of his setting hens. During the incubation period I built several spacious cages in one of my old sheds. I wound up with eight cock birds and two hens out of the original clutch of ten eggs. The hens were free to roam, but the cock birds had to be separated and put into individual cages. The long waiting process began.

It takes a couple of years before obtaining the desirable quality of feathers, and during this period there are apt to be numerous problems. There are no guarantees. In fact, out of the eight cock birds, only two of them had real promise with regards to color. But, as luck would have it, after a year and a half of caring devotion, I found both of my gems lying belly-up from natural causes. They succumbed within two months of each other. Of course, the other birds with less desirable colors lived long and happily. After the last bird met his maker, I promised to leave the bird-raising to Harry. I kept my promise.

Another feather in great demand and equally hard to come by was the flank feather of the male wood duck. If you were a Catskill fisherman, the lemon flank feather in combination with dun hackle was, in essence, the staff of life. Dyed mallard was readily available but, at best, it lacked the well-defined texture and appearance of the genuine feather. Unless you were a duck hunter or knew one, this feather was extremely difficult to obtain.

Earlier in life I had done a considerable amount of duck shooting, but my quarry were predominately the other puddlers—black ducks and mallards. Once in a while, a Canada goose would come my way, and perhaps an occasional wood duck or green-winged teal as a bonus. Fortunately, I lived in an area that abounded with good, wood duck habitat. Both sides of the Hudson River Valley in New York State had good cover, with many meandering rivers flowing through adjacent swamps. It took a lot of research and mulling over topo maps to put it all together, but in time, with a lot of leg work, I put a plan into action.

The first task was to build myself a small duck boat, one that was light enough to transport and easy enough for one person to handle. I also wanted reliable safety features. Stability is necessary when handling a shotgun in a small boat. A canoe, with one man paddling in the stern and the shooter in the bow, is fine for a joint hunt, but much of my duck hunting would be a solo affair. My craft would have to be capable of being either paddled or rowed, and have balance when I needed to drop the oars and reach for the gun.

I spent a good part of the summer putting the little plywood duck boat together. When finished and camouflaged with marsh-green paint, the flat-bottomed boat measured seven feet in length. It was a little heavy, but manageable, and it fit nicely into the back of my station wagon.

That fall, I floated a small river prior to the opening of duck season. The shakedown cruise ran smoothly. Now I would spend most of my time securing access to hunting sites. In those days, posting land was not in vogue as it is today and obtaining permission to hunt was relatively easy.

Wood ducks are early migrators. They arrive early in the Hudson Valley and leave early. They are long gone by freeze-up. I put all my efforts into the early season, when the birds were most plentiful. Mornings and evenings were devoted to the swamps, when the birds were most active. The afternoons were spent floating rivers and jump-shooting birds from my duck boat. Like fishing a new trout stream, exploration of these rivers became a joy in itself. Most exciting were the sounds of whistling wings overhead, invisible birds shrouded by the fog-laden river as I wound my way slowly through the swamps.

I remember one particular trip when I couldn't see the birds through the dense mist, but could hear them land with splashes on a large pool below me. I quietly lifted the oar and gently paddled slowly through the mist. When I arrived where the wood ducks had landed, I saw nothing. They had evaporated into the dense growth. Then, just behind me, with an explosion of wings, six birds burst from a small backwater. The report of my double echoed down the valley. Curved feathers drifted onto the dark pool. I paddled to the far bank and retrieved two birds, adult males in exquisite color.

These events would repeat themselves over the years. There were misses, of course, plenty of them, but over a period of time my collection grew considerably.

Even today, years later, when I browse through the old wooden trunk and see those flank feathers, the pungent smell of spent gunpowder still lingers in a morning mist.

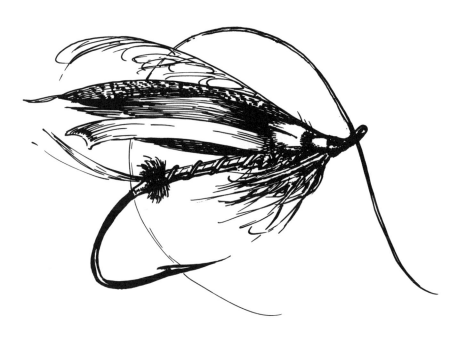

More Feathers

Back in the late 1950s within the shadows of Manhattan, I joined a small group of anglers who agreed to meet one night a week so that both accomplished and novice fly tyers could share fly tying techniques in an informal setting. Through the efforts of the Southern New York Fish and Game Association (a Westchester County rod and gun club), space was obtained in one of the rooms at the county center in White Plains, New York. This was twenty-odd miles north of the big city and was centralized enough for all to be involved. We met on Thursday evenings.

As I look back now, I wonder how many of the new tyers realized their good fortune when their mentors included Keith Fulsher, originator of the Thunder Creek series of flies, and Chuck Conrad, whose Atlantic hair wing salmon flies were popular on Canadian salmon rivers. Congenial Irv Lacey, puffing on his pipe, was at the helm, encouraging the newcomers and complimenting them on their achievements. Bob Sigsby was there, and so was that remarkable feather merchant and good friend of Ray Bergman, Herb Howard. Who could forget that little smile on Herb's face after he performed a piece of finger magic by winging a salmon fly or turning a pair of hackles on a dry fly?

Herb was the unofficial supplier of feathers and materials. Each week he would arrive with an old suitcase filled with fly tying delights. It was a good opportunity to purchase feathers firsthand, and new tyers would receive an education on the attributes of various materials (what to look for in quality necks, etc.). Necks were number one in demand, and Herb had every color, size, and shape available.

There were creams, browns, grizzly, furnace, black, white. And if he didn't have it, one just asked for what was wanted and the request would be filled by the following week. High on the list were Herb's own specially dyed Blue Dun necks. They were the best that I've ever used. By the way, the cost of the necks ran from $1.00 to $2.50 for standard colors, and $3.00 for the dyed dun necks.

It was about this time that Herb began experimenting with his pre-waxed fly tying thread so popular with fly tyers today. Every week he would come in with wooden spools of thread with an "improved" wax formula that would become "more improved" and finally perfected. The original thread came with a small disk of additional wax attached to the side of the spool. He relied on the wax adhesion to secure the materials and could wing a fly with as few turns as possible. I never saw Herb use a bobbin when he tied flies.

In addition to the pre-waxed thread, Herb also made excellent hackle pliers. Using quality spring wire, a bench vise and a large file, he turned out the pliers quickly and precisely. I have several pairs of these hackle pliers that are forty years old and still going strong.

When Herb passed away, a private sale was held in the basement of his home in Mamaroneck, New York. Four-by-eight sheets of plywood were mounted on wooden horses filling the entire downstairs space. Placed on the tables was a lifetime accumulation of fly tying materials, hooks, and fishing tackle. It was one of the largest personal collections I have ever seen.

As time went by, the fly tying sessions proved to be very successful. They were so popular that they became one of the main attractions at the rod and gun club's booth at the annual Sportsman's Show in New York City held in late February. This was the only show in town devoted to hunting and fishing. There were no shows devoted purely to fly fishing in those days. It was a welcome tonic to weary minds

An angler's decision—dry fly or wet fly?

tired of a grueling gray winter. It gave most of us a chance to see familiar angling faces and pick up a few fly tying materials from dealers at the show. These early shows had a more personalized feeling and a congeniality that seems to be lacking in today's high tech "guaranteed" style.

The shows had interesting casting events, both fly and bait, and even then there were celebrity exhibitions. Ellis Newman would demonstrate his ability to fly cast for both distance and accuracy. The unique thing about Ellis was that he did not use a fly rod, but cast his line by hand. Baseball great Ted Williams and former heavyweight boxing champ Jack Sharkey would engage in friendly fly casting duels. All of this was going on while northern lumberjacks were building a log cabin and staging log-rolling contests in a huge water tank. The scent of pine permeated the Maine exhibit while anglers dreamed of hooking the large landlocked salmon and brook trout that swam in the artificial, woodland pool.

The long, fly tying table at the booth was manned by the club tyers. We tied flies for visiting sportsmen and sportswomen. A small donation box was placed in the middle of the table, and all proceeds went to the club. We had numerous guest tyers. Charlie DeFeo stands out foremost in my memory. His artistic abilities, combined with his thorough knowledge of feathers, produced the finest Atlantic salmon flies—absolute perfection.

Considering the historical value of the tyers and their flies, a small fortune must be lying in some old fly books of visitors who dropped coins in that donation box.

Several years later, the enthusiasm of the tyers grew even more. In addition to our Thursday night sessions, we began to assemble at the workshop of rod-maker George Halstead on Sunday afternoons. We tied flies and cast rods nonstop. It was about this time that fisherman, fly tyer, and photographer Mattie Vinceguerra joined us and showed us some of his patterns that were developed on the East Branch of the Croton River.

Tragically, our Sunday meetings at Halstead's ended one late winter day when George, always thoughtful of his fellow anglers, chose to lay wood planks on a wet, mud-soaked walkway that led to his shop. While constructing the walkway he collapsed. He died on the way to the hospital. The world lost a fine rod maker, considered by many to be far ahead of his time in rod design and tapers. His ferrules were simply the best.

There is an interesting footnote to be added to the story of this small gathering of fly tyers and their devotion to flies and fish: they were among the first angler/conservationists in New York State to encourage the implementation of artificial lure-only regulations on selected waters. I wrote an article entitled "Look to the Future" for the Southern New York Sportsmen's magazine that spearheaded a drive to make the Amawalk Outlet one of the first rivers in southern New York to be designated artificial lure only. Nearly forty years later, the regulations are still in effect.

A traditional outing.

Endangered Species

There is a form of fly fishing that is like a spent spinner, fading and dying. Its roots extend probably as far back as fly fishing itself. The venerable winged wet fly, once popular and a staple in a trout fisher's fly book, has lost favor.

Angling catalogues, once filled with hundreds of time-honored wet fly trout patterns, have reduced their selection to a mere two or three. I suppose fly tyers, in their endeavor to imitate every subsurface insect exactly, had much to do with it. In the process of eliminating many of the "near enough" wet fly patterns, they have also discontinued attractor patterns that continue to work magic on rivers and still waters today.

Slowly fading, too, is a breed of wet fly practitioners that cast their flies with unrivaled style and grace. One can only recollect that special cadre of fishermen, the likes of Jim Leisenring, Ed Sens, Ray Smith, and Herman Christian, to mention a few, who elevated wet fly fishing to an art form.

Fully aware of its versatility, they cast their flies with confidence on Catskill rivers and the flowing streams of Pennsylvania. They paid little attention to the "great debate" circulating among fly fishers as to how one should fish upstream with a dry fly or downstream with a wet fly. They were practical fishermen, fishing both ways and refusing to involve themselves with extreme, dogmatic theories as long as fly angling remained within the realm of normal fly fishing practice. In principle it made sense. The wet fly was pivotal, considering the fact that the major portion of a trout's diet is beneath the surface.

Many of the creations in larger sizes might well imitate a larger nymph, or perhaps a small baitfish. In miniature sizes they resembled emerging nymphs, drowned mayfly duns, submerged terrestrials, and a host of other insects that drifted through the riffles, runs and pools of classic trout waters. Skillful, wet fly fishermen were quick to realize this and created fly patterns accordingly, including wet downwing imitations of popular dry flies such as Quill Gordon, Cahill, Hendrickson, etc. All that glitters is not gold, and all feeding trout are not top water feeding fish, even though they may be seen breaking the surface.

Many creations, dubbed with lovely names worthy of a poet's gift, were exquisitely tied. I have a set of flies (William Mills and Son, circa early 1900s) tied on snells that are abso-

Simple wet flies, an endangered species.

lutely beautiful. They are tied with delicate and transparent wing quills, a single turn of hackle, a slender body, a few wisps for a tail, and the tiniest head. I would defy even the harshest of critics to doubt their trout-taking abilities, even on today's heavily-fished waters.

When an angler's thoughts retreat to northern waters and eastern brook trout, the "bright-fly page" of his fly book is opened. What enchanting names: Parmachenee Belle, Queen O' Waters, Alexandra, Lady of the Lake. Hardly soiled doves, their allure is as genuine as their names imply. They have been seducing *Fontinalis* for over a century.

To deny fly tiers new horizons in their creativity would be wrong. Equally wrong would be the discarding of our angling heritage because these flies failed to meet true-to-life criteria. The last vestige of hope remains with downwing-feathered Atlantic salmon and steelhead wet flies, which are still in use today. They are cast upstream and allowed to dead drift, or cast down and across, allowing the fly to swing through the current. This glimmer of hope may someday revive the time-honored tradition of wading a trout stream casting a single or a brace of feather-winged wet flies on bright waters.

Brook Trout: Medicine Places

There is a time and a place for all things. In the world of angling, the mood is set by the surroundings. If you are wading an Atlantic salmon river where the rewards are high in hopes but few in fish, you prepare yourself for a long siege of arduous casting. It may be days before a fish will roll to your fly. The stakes are high and feelings run electric. It is big water, big tackle, and big fish.

The same can be said of fishing for steelhead fresh from open water. The angler must again prepare himself for a lengthy campaign. He needs strong tackle and plenty of backing to handle the long runs through the pools and rapids before this noble fish is vanquished and lying on the beach.

Behold the brook trout, the little jewel of secluded waters. Whether it be a remote, northern pond or a small mountain brook, the wild squaretail is found only in pristine waters. This prerequisite will send you on a voyage to wilderness places where the surroundings themselves are the tonic needed to keep your keel even in an uneven world. These haunts are best described by Native Americans as medicine places ... and they are.

In the northern ponds you can listen to the distant call of the loons as you cast your flies into the waters beneath white birch and northern spruce. On the bigger water, where pond food is more plentiful, the flanks of the squaretail are well rounded. And it is here, in a canoe, fly fishing a chain of wilderness ponds, that an angler can feel the magic of solitude. Among the dimpling rises, your company might include a diving osprey, moose feeding on water plants, or the thunderous crack of a beaver's tail.

I have often felt that an environment like this should be where all anglers learn to fly fish. The refinements of tackle and its usage will come in time, but for now, in the hands of a down-to-earth, observant woodsman, one learns to appreciate the absolute beauty that surrounds the world of angling. Fishing is more than catching fish, and it is unfortunate that many poor souls angling today never enter passage beyond the initial obsession of getting fish.

A long trip, and sleeping nights out beneath the stars, is strongly recommended. There should be a small fire for company and a few, wild brook trout split and broiled over a bed of hot coals. To fall asleep, all you need is the sound of wavelets gently lapping the shoreline of your wilderness camp.

The time of year will dictate your choice of flies. Streamers, bucktails, and big, wet flies fished fairly deep will do well early in the season after the ice breaks up. If there are smelt running the rivers in early spring, careful casting at the mouth of a brook should yield a few swirls. The old traditional patterns, tied in various sizes, have withstood the test of time and are as effective today as they were fifty years ago. The Gray Ghost, Nine-Three, and the Supervisor are good smelt patterns. The Light and Dark Edson Tigers and the Barnes Special are good attractors.

I prefer a long cane rod, eight-and-one-half to nine feet in length, when fly-casting from the canoe. This allows for a higher backcast while sitting. A nine or ten-foot leader, tapered to 1x or 2x, is about right for the bigger flies. If you decide to drop down to a smaller size fly, you can add a thinner strand of tippet material. For casting, a number six or eight streamer hook works well.

Trolling a streamer fly off the mouths of brooks and gravel bars can be very effective. Smelt will run the brooks at night and big squaretails will follow them. A thirty to forty-foot leader attached to a sinking fly line is a fine starter. I prefer a level leader of six or eight-pound test. To the end of this I'll tie on a number two to six size streamer or bucktail. If the smelt run large, the tandem fly is an excellent choice. My own experience has proven that the fish run somewhat larger on the long flies. Should your fly ride the surface when trolling, it may be necessary to add some weight two feet above the fly. It is also a good plan to keep two rods in the canoe should you decide to fly cast. This will save time when you are changing leaders or spooling in a trolling line.

After a trout has been hooked and played, landing the fish should be a simple affair. Use a long-handled canoe net. Leave the small stream net at home, for it serves no practical purpose when reaching over the gunwale to net a trout. A long-handled net with a large hoop and strong mesh netting is ideal. Another choice is the collapsible, triangular-shaped net that has an adjustable extension handle.

In late spring and early summer, trout will begin to take flies on the surface of the pond as winged insects begin to appear. Speaking of winged insects, some of the best squaretail fishing is found in the month of June. In northern waters it is also prime black fly time. In numbers there is strength, and these little hellions are unified beyond belief. Their persistence can make the strongest of men flee the woods in total madness. A prolonged wet spring may also increase the mosquito population, adding more grief to the matter. There is some relief if you are on open water with a few breezes blowing enough to scatter these little demons, but rest assured that peril awaits you when you beach your canoe. The humming in the spruce thickets are mosquitoes bent on getting their pound of flesh.

Several years ago, my wife and I were fishing Adirondack waters during the height of the black fly season. No angler could ask for a better companion, for she is as adept at handling a fly rod as any man I know. She has trekked many trails with our Oldtown canoe on her shoulders, but her fair skin, and some mysterious natural attractant that she possesses is a beacon of light for those little devils. By the end of the first day, welts began to show behind her ears and down her neck. Then the fever began. She was forced to abandon her fishing, and rest. She insisted on staying, so I went into town and located a head net and some medication. By the next day she was in good spirits and we continued fishing. The remainder of the trip was problem-free.

Thus forewarned of spring and its pesky insects, your dry fly fishing can be one of the most enjoyable ways of hooking trout early in the season. It is advisable to have your guide or partner paddle you into the best possible casting position as you approach rising fish. A capable canoe handler who knows how to fish is a godsend when you are in the bow delivering line. The accomplished paddler has a sixth sense in knowing how to position the canoe accurately.

Trout cruising the pond can be ready takers, or damnably difficult when they become selective. Fast-water river fish can be child's play compared to bringing cruising trout to the fly. For the most part, a trout feeding in fast-moving currents must hit quickly or go hungry. This can be to an angler's advantage. A good presentation and a reasonable fly selection will usually bring the feeding fish up to the fly.

On the other hand, a pond trout can inspect your fly all day long if he cares to. On quiet water, a small twitch of the rod will put enough movement on the fly, often triggering a pass. This works well when casting towards the shoreline. The dry fly is checked in flight, allowing it to drift down lightly on the surface. A small flick of the wrist is all that is needed to make the fly dance. Then pause, allowing the fly to rest for a few moments.

Variants, Skaters, and Spider flies are very well suited for this type of fishing. The long length of the hackles allows these flies to tumble on the surface just enough to represent a struggling insect.

Unless you fish a pond daily, predicting hatches is a rather "iffy" affair. A pond can come alive with trout gorging themselves on insects well into the dark of the evening. With a little luck, you might find fish working again the next evening. Then the whole affair can turn off as quickly as it began, and you would proclaim to the world that this pond never saw the fin of a trout.

A working knowledge of an individual pond should acquaint you with most of its natural flies during the course of a season. When a hatch occurs, it is wise to have a fair selection of imitations in your fly book. If you have them in various sizes, so much the better. Standard dry fly patterns,

The "little salmon of the fountain."

either quill-wing, no-wing, or hair wing, should suffice, along with various midge patterns. So much of this fishing depends upon water conditions, be it wind-rippled or glass-like.

The angler's idyllic world consists of huge trout rolling on a number twelve or fourteen well-balanced fly. This makes perfect sense from an angler's point of view, but all too often not to a trout's eye. For some reason known only to fish, they may bypass the larger insects and cruise the pond devouring all the minutiae they can find. This can shatter the confidence of the most disciplined angler. Sometimes, a few adjustments can help. The leader can be lengthened and the finest of tippet material added, along with a smaller fly. A long line is usually best, and the fly should descend softly ahead of the cruising fish. You will be better off picking out one fish, as opposed to throwing your fly out indiscriminately. It is much like swinging a gun on an individual bird, as opposed to shooting blindly into the entire covey.

Sometimes even the best attempts may prove futile, but that is the nature of the game. A wise angler once put it quite aptly: "The only certain thing about fishing is the uncertainty of it all." He must have been sitting in the middle of a smooth-surfaced pond, suffering the indignities of refusal.

An alternate way of taking these trout when the dry fly fails is to fish the wet fly beneath the surface. Cast the fly ahead of a feeding fish, allowing it to sink several inches, and then retrieve it, stripping the line steadily. Look for that telltale boil and feel the gentle tug as the trout strikes the fly.

At times, particularly when the water is calm, it can be difficult to sink a wet fly. A floating fly line and a nylon leader can hamper attempts to get the fly under the surface. Your options include a preparation applied to the leader and fly to make them sink, or changing to a sinking fly line. When purchasing a sinking line, I would recommend a dark-colored line. If the fish can see a white-winged Royal Coachman coming through the water, then it will certainly be able to see forty or fifty feet of white fly line in front of it.

The traditional wet fly patterns, numbering in the hundreds, if not thousands, can be found in any of the older fly-pattern books and can offer the most discerning angler an unlimited choice of flies. A pair of wet flies fished together can also be effective. A small Black Gnat, a Gold-Ribbed Hare's Ear, or a Leadwing Coachman as a tail fly are good choices. A Campbell's Fancy, or perhaps a Royal Coachman, are good dropper flies. I prefer to use a somber-colored fly as the tail fly, and a more colorful fly as the dropper. The dropper fly is tied about eighteen inches above the lower fly. The trick is to keep the dropper leader short, about four to five inches. The shorter the dropper leader, the less chance it has of twisting around the main leader. The dropper leader should also be 1x or 2x larger than the main tippet. If the dropper leader is looped, it is quite easy to remove the fly, should you wish to cast a single fly.

As the weather warms, brook trout seek cooler water temperatures. In ponds, this means spring holes. These are cold water seepages rising from the bottom of the pond. To the angler, it means getting the fly down to the fish. In fairly shallow ponds, the fly line is cast out and allowed to sink to the fishes' level. It is important to be patient and allow the necessary time for the line to sink down deep enough, whether the choice is a big wet fly, nymph, or streamer.

Several years ago I fished an Adirondack pond in late September. The maples displayed their reds and golds, and the yellow leaves of the white birches were a vibrant contrast against a backdrop of green hemlocks. I had fished a single streamer in and out of several coves with nothing save a half-hearted swirl from an undersized fish. The cool nights of the past week were beginning to lower the water temperature, but not enough to suit the comfort of fall-colored brook trout.

I paddled the canoe a short distance to where a series of rock ledges fell sharply into the water. It was fifteen feet deep, with a cold water spring at the bottom. I put on a number eight wet fly, let it sink, and then began to retrieve it ever so slowly. On the third strip of the line, I felt a strike. The rod bent as the fish pulled line. The trout dug deeper with a series of fierce headshakes. Before long, I could see a glint of gold as the fish rose from the depths. He gave me a gallant fight, and when it was over I slipped my net beneath the surface and old speckles was secure in the linen mesh. It was a fourteen-inch male in brilliant fall colors, sporting a small kype.

Fishing the rise.

Within the next hour I hooked and released eight more trout, the largest a shade over sixteen inches. Quite content with my good fortune, for curiosity's sake I fished in ever widening circles beyond the spring hole. The warmer water yielded no fish. Moving back into the spring area, I continued casting and picked up a few more brook trout. Locating fish in the colder water, experimenting with fly patterns, and a little patience had proven successful. On this day, I did well on a big wet fly.

While on the subject of wet flies, many of the old favorites, including the Montreal, Silver Doctor, and the Parmachenee Belle (queen of all brook trout flies), still perform well for brook trout on northern waters. I like them either alone or fished as a dropper fly.

Mr. Henry P. Wells first tied the Parmachenee Belle, during the late nineteenth century, in the Rangely Lakes section of Maine. He created a legacy that is still carried on today by the faithful, despite the fact that today's angling catalogs list only a fraction of the wet fly patterns that were advertised thirty or forty years ago. I suppose winging a wet fly is time consuming for some fly tyers, and it is easier to tie the more current wingless flies; nevertheless, it is quite pleasing to me to see the old Parma Belle in the lip of a squaretail. These old flies are time machines. May the tradition continue as long as a fly is cast on brook trout waters.

Along The Way

Fly fishing and hunting have much in common. To anyone who has waded miles of rivers and tramped across mountain ridges, the sixth sense of forecasting the day's results is amazingly accurate. The veteran deer hunter "feels" the woods; he knows when conditions are right. The wind is favorable, so is the footing, and deer movement is at its peak. He may not slay his buck that day, but he knows he will see deer. The same goes for the seasoned fisherman. He, also, "feels" the pulse of the river. The weather, water level, temperature, and water clarity are good indicators, as are insect activity and a score of other factors that filter through a mind that has analyzed these situations time and time again. Between success and disappointment lie the flukes, the unexplained, and even the humorous aspects of sports afield.

One June evening, I had a telephone call from Frank Mele inviting me to join him and a lady friend on a daytime fishing trip to the Delaware River. His friend, Hideko, the mother of one of his violin students, had taken a keen interest in fly fishing. She had sought Frank's expertise in angling, and he had given her several lessons in fly casting. With further guidance, she purchased several fine cane rods, quality reels, and some excellent dry fly patterns tied personally by Art Flick at his Westkill home. She took to fly fishing ... period!

We met Saturday morning at Frank's home in Woodstock, packed our gear and lunch in the car, and departed for the far side of the Catskills. The trip there (as all fishing trips are) was full of excitement, anticipation, and optimistic banter. En route, Frank and I reminisced about his youthful fishing days in western New York and of his friendship with rod-maker Dan Brenan. We shared stories of Catskill fishing experiences on the East Branch and Beaver Kill rivers.

The Delaware River below Hancock was perfect that day. Cool air moved down the valley and tiny mayflies drifted like little sailboats down the huge pools, called "eddies" in this part of the country.

Almost immediately, I saw Frank's rod straining. His favorite Payne bobbed as he played a heavy fish. After a long fight, he carefully landed and released an eighteen-inch brown trout—a dark fish, well marked.

Moving up to the next pool, I caught and released several rainbows—not very large, but certainly big in spirit. Glancing upriver I could see Hideko's rod at work. She was getting into fish. In fact, every time I looked, her little Constable cane rod was busy. She was netting one fish after another.

Later that day, one by one, we arrived back at the car to have a late afternoon lunch. Frank and I arrived first and shared our day's experiences.

In the distance, we could see Hideko making her way carefully along the path at river's edge. She waved and we could tell by the expression on her face that, undoubtedly, good fortune had befallen her. We eagerly awaited her report. Smiling and excited, she told us of a wonderful day's fishing, imitating flies, stalking fish, and catching one trout after another. She had kept only the largest. Proudly, she lifted open the top of her willow creel and exposed them for our approval. There, on the bottom of the basket, neatly arranged on a bed of green ferns, lay five of the biggest silver chubs you could ever imagine!

One afternoon, Keith Fulsher and I had been discussing his Thundercreek flies and assorted fly tying techniques. At the end of our conversation, I casually mentioned that fishing on the Esopus had been good, and if he had the time, I might be able to get him into a few rainbows. He agreed.

Early June weather is normally pleasant in the Catskills, but that day was unusually cold. A few, scattered Gray Foxes were hatching when we arrived on the river. Several small fish in the tail of the pool made some half-hearted rises, but nothing too serious was happening. We put our rods together and waited. It did not take long. Tan caddis flies began to make their appearances, slowly at first, but steadily increasing, until fish, always opportunistic, began swiping the caddis before they reached the surface.

As the evening wore on and the hatch increased, even the most selective fish became reckless, slashing the caddis as they broke the surface film. A small twitch of a caddis imitation riding the current was all that was necessary to turn a fish.

We waded into the river and began casting to rising fish. Almost immediately Keith raised and hooked a "reel-screamer." I could see his white fly line scissoring the surface as a big rainbow headed downriver. Ten minutes later, an eighteen-inch fish lay on the gravel bar. We dispatched the fish, put it in a large, woven basket, and placed it about thirty paces into the river on a huge flat boulder. We returned to our fishing.

The evening passed quickly. Dusk approached, that time of day when the dark tones of the river surroundings blend in harmony with a starlit sky. I was about to make my last cast, when I noticed an object floating by the boulder where the basket was stashed. It resembled a half-submerged log broken free from an upstream logjam. Then I looked again. The log was walking on top of our boulder. It was a big raccoon. That rascal had sniffed out our stash from the bank and was helping himself to a free dinner.

I waved my arms, uttered some choice phrases, and quickly made tracks for the bank. It is one thing to wade a slippery river in daylight, but charging through dark waters is impossible. By the time I approached the rock, the beggar was on the bank, his prize tightly clenched in his jaws. He paused to shake dripping water from his rotund body. I picked up the empty basket, realizing my attempted recovery was futile. By this time Keith had joined me. We searched in the lengthening shadows, squinting as we moved forward on hands and knees. The narrow beam of light from the flashlight revealed only wet paw prints accompanied by a fishy odor. To continue the chase any longer was wishful thinking. We returned to the riverbank, gathered our gear, and prepared to depart. Suddenly, both of us broke out into laughter. You know the kind I mean—when your stomach hurts so much it's difficult to breathe.

Somewhere, in the cavernous hollow of a decaying tree, a masked bandit was sharing dinner with relatives. When the feast had ended, I'm sure there followed huge grins and the licking of little paws.

Were we duped? You bet we were!

Spring had been very dry. Rains that normally fell in April and May were far short of expectations. The Ashokan Reservoir was low, and the last pool on the Esopus ended at Twin Rocks, a third of a mile below the high-water mark.

Little rainbow trout were cruising in the backwaters, sipping mayflies stalled in white clouds of foam. If you could present your fly properly, it was not difficult to raise a fish. They were small trout, but offered lots of sport.

After a short lunch break that left the pool well rested, I picked a fresh Dun Variant from my box and attached it to my tippet. I put it over the first rising trout. It was a small fish. He poked his nose out of the water, swallowed the fly, and gave a few short runs followed by little skittering bursts across the surface as I brought him in.

A dozen feet from where I stood in the current, an enormous rock lay a foot and a half below the surface. While retrieving the rainbow, I noticed a large, dark shadow appearing over the submerged rock. Then I saw it—a huge brown trout, at least an eight to ten-pounder. With lightning speed he grabbed my little rainbow sideways in his jaws. I felt the sheer weight of the fish as my rod tip lunged forward. This locomotive turned easily and steamed confidently towards the reservoir. My reel started with a basso tone, then, with quick acceleration, the pitch became higher and higher. As the reel screamed and the line cut through the water, I had flashbacks of Atlantic salmon fishing. When my backing began to follow the line, I headed for the dry cobblestone bank and followed the fish downstream in quick pursuit.

For whatever reason, calmness came over me and I began to chuckle. It occurred to me that this entire scenario could end abruptly if my leviathan were to simply open his mouth and let go of his prey. Sure enough, with a final whirrrrrr of the reel, the line went slack. He was gone. All that remained was my fly hanging at the end of the tippet.

As I reeled in my line, a question entered my mind, one that deserves reflection. I shall pass it on for your generous consideration.

Suppose this had been fly-only water (which it was not), and suppose that I had successfully landed that big brown trout with a fly-hooked rainbow dangling from his mouth.

Remember now ... how often on eastern rivers will an angler take a fish of these proportions on a fly? For many, this would be a once-in-a-lifetime experience.

Would the fish have been taken legally on a fly, or would it have been taken illegally on bait? Would I have had possession with clear conscience, or would I have been reduced to possession and *forget* conscience? Hmmm.

What would *you* have done?

The Unexplained

The trials of everyday life are put aside when an angler reaches for a fly rod and departs for bright waters, but there are times when the overlapping of the two worlds becomes unavoidable.

There is a tradition in my world that compels me to give homage to recently departed angling friends. Unfortunately, the older I become, the more I am called upon to perform this solemn obligation. The ritual is simple enough. The first trout of the year taken on a dry fly is dedicated to a departed friend. After a few seconds of silence, the fish is released. I snip off the fly and float it downriver with the current into a watery world that once held friendship together with a common bond—fly fishing.

Sometimes, at least in my life, incidents occur that possess an air of mysticism and offer no easy explanation. Maybe they are best left unexplained ...

Footsteps

It was fall, the time of year to gather feathers. Back home in the Catskills this never presented a problem, for I knew the local swamps well, and duck shooting was fairly predictable. Now, after a temporary relocation to New England, my spare time was spent exploring the local countryside searching for small bogs and swamps that might harbor wood ducks.

On my new terrain I found a few choice spots, but there was one bog that really looked promising. Actually, there were two bodies of water joined together by a shallow, meandering river that flowed through pin oaks for several hundred yards. The open hardwood stood tall with grassy hummocks and low alders bordering the riverbanks. There were several bends in the river with a few, fair-sized pools adjacent to the turns. These were good places to jump-shoot ducks during the middle of the day.

It was mid-October when I decided to carry out my plan and give the river a trial run. I parked my car at the end of an old logging road not far from the lower bog. From there, I could wade the river upstream fairly easily.

As I put my waders on, I couldn't help but think of the rivers back home and all those wonderful float trips in years gone by. How many times, by wading slowly and quietly, had I jumped ducks at twenty yards, picked out the drakes as they lifted, and left the rest to my old side-by-side?

The leaves were dry on this warm fall day. It would be impossible to walk the bank quietly for a better view. I slipped into the river and filled the tubes with a pair of shells. Fifty yards upstream were the remnants of an old beaver dam. As I approached it, two birds rose quickly, but I held up. I had a good see on the last bird, a hen. I never saw the first one as they both exited with that unforgettable *weep-weep-weep*. The sound was welcome; I had found some woodies.

I poked around the dried-up beaver pond looking for a hidden pothole, but never found one. Returning to the little river, I continued to move upstream. After wading thirty yards, I saw two birds lift from the bank, clearing the alders. I shouldered the double and the right choke found its mark, an adult male. I retrieved the bird and sat down on an old log to admire it. The green crest on its head was iridescent against the sunlit river. There were many Fanwing Coachmans on the breast and, of course, Quill Gordons and salmon flies under the wings. I celebrated the occasion with a small cup of coffee from my thermos, picked up the empty shell, and slipped the bird into the back of my jacket.

From there, the river widened and became rather shallow. The tall oaks thinned out. Looking into the woods, my view was clear for two hundred yards. I had taken about ten paces upriver when I heard faint footsteps coming from the direction of the trees. I turned, looked, but could see nothing. Could it be another hunter? No. Perhaps it was a deer? No, it couldn't be a deer. I had heard that pause in whitetail movement too many times before.

The steady shuffling and the crunch of dry leaves was that of another person, coming closer and closer, yet I could not see anyone. I stepped out of the river for a better view, but there was no one there. The steps were so near; it was as though someone were passing directly in front of me. I gave a faint, "hello," then a little louder, "HELLO!" There was no reply. The footsteps turned and began to fade away. They evaporated into the oaks, leaving only silence. I stared into the woods for ten minutes, maybe longer, trying to make sense of this mystery. Lacking answers, I tried to shrug the whole thing off, turned back to the river, and continued the hunt. I glanced at my watch. It was twelve o'clock noon.

I moved slowly, anticipating a flush of birds, but could not forget those footsteps. At the next bend of the river, four woodies reached for the sky, but I was unable to concentrate and never managed to get the gun up in time. I decided to call it quits.

Walking back downriver towards the wood road, I passed the site where the unexplained had happened. Despite feeling uneasy, I paused for one last glance. The woods remained undisturbed. I headed back to the car, put my gun and coat in the trunk, and drove home.

When I pulled into the driveway, I was greeted by my dog, always anxious to see me and even more interested in sniffing the contents of my hunting jacket. I gave him some gentle pats on the head and opened the front door. I immediately had the feeling that something was wrong. It was the sensation one gets when the phone rings at two in the morning. The inevitable phrase followed: "Sit down. I have something to tell you."

A phone call had come just a short time before my arrival. A very close loved one had passed away. He had died at twelve o'clock noon. They wanted me to be the first to know.

All I could hear were footsteps on the dry leaves.

Charlie

I had known Charlie since our early school days. We fished the Catskills together, perhaps not as often as we had hoped for, but the times spent on the rivers were always pleasant. He was a good companion.

The Schoharie and the Esopus Creek were our main haunts, and it was on these waters that our flies probed every pool and rapid. We were successful, as I recall—not too many large fish, but plenty of creel-size browns and rainbows.

At day's end, we would stow away our fishing gear, roll out our sleeping bags, and camp along the riverbank. A small fire would keep us company. In those days it was common to drive down an old road to the river's edge and do this. As long as you minded your own business and respected property, no one would bother you.

After dinner we would talk fishing, flies, and share all of those wonderful stories of stream lore. I'm sure we caught and lost more fish during those fireside evenings than we ever caught in all our actual travels. Invariably, we would open a small flask and toast all those Catskill anglers past who had cast their flies on these grand old waters. Quite often, as we reminisced, Charlie would reach into his shirt pocket and produce a pack of Chesterfield cigarettes that he kept in a handmade leather case. We would talk long into the night, and I can still see the glow of his lit cigarette well after the embers had died out. As a matter of fact, those

Chesterfields became Charlie's trademark. He always had several packs lying on the front seat of his car, and his workshop floor was strewn with field-stripped white cigarette papers.

Besides being a good fisherman, Charlie was a fine photographer. He became the official recorder of events whenever an occasion would arise—weddings, banquets, etc. He was also a fine carpenter and cabinetmaker. When my fly tying room became a disaster with fur and feathers stuffed into every box and jar I could find, it was Charlie who suggested he make a fly tying desk to organize the chaos. He did, and forty years later it is still with me. He also built a beautiful, wooden tackle box, with brass hardware, that houses an abundant supply of fly tackle.

I suppose that it was only natural that as we got older, the everyday involvement with work and family obligations would limit the amount of time we could spend together. On rare occasions, we would meet and talk of the old days. With a little luck, we would spend evenings chasing a few rainbows on the Esopus. At dusk, in the distance, I would see the glow of his cigarette.

The times together were limited, and the hours spent wading our beloved rivers became fewer and fewer. Weeks grew into months, and months into years. Commitments and distance separated us. Time passed, and we were both middle-aged.

I had just finished a business trip, and with thoughts of giving the river a few casts before dark, I went into my tackle room to rummage through some gear. The phone rang and I answered it. An old friend told me that Charlie had suffered a terrible accident. After taking the last series of photographs of a wedding, Charlie had backed up against the steps of the church and tripped, his head hitting the concrete. He had lost consciousness. The ambulance took him to the hospital, where two hours later he was pronounced dead. I was shocked. I hung up the phone and sat there with that sinking feeling one gets when death becomes reality.

I stared out the window, gazing at the small brook that flows by the house. Turning the clock back, I could see Charlie's smiling face as he displayed a fine fish he had just taken. All of the memories returned: the pools, the runs, the rapids, and those starlit nights by the campfire.

When the shock of the news lifted, I took a rod from the corner of the room and a reel from the old wooden tackle box, and headed for the Bend Pool, one that Charlie and I had fished together many times. Starting with a dry fly at the run below the pool, I worked my way upstream. A fish or two may have come to my fly, I really don't recall. I left the run, skirting the fast water, and walked along the cobblestone bank. Just before reaching the Bend Pool I noticed a white object lying on the stones, about six inches from the water's edge. When I picked it up, a chill came over my body and a rush of cold air swept by me. I was holding an empty pack of Chesterfield cigarettes.

Hooked ... Hold him gently.

Harry

I had just fished my way down through a stretch of fast water. Several small trout had come to a number ten Dark Cahill wet fly, but all of them had turned short. The water below me narrowed and picked up speed before entering the big pool beneath the old, iron bridge.

I began lengthening fly line across the water, when I noticed a car slowly edging its way to the side of the bridge. An elderly fellow, tall, with a distinguished pencil moustache, got out of the car and casually made his way to the center of the bridge. He stopped, crouched over the railing, and gazed into the pool. His hands acted as blinders as he searched the water below. The old gent moved a few steps backward, took a harder look into the water and, waving his arms, gained my attention. He pointed his finger to one side of the abutment beneath him. Trying to keep his voice as low as possible, he said, "A good trout is feeding just under the surface, taking nymphs no doubt."

I took a few cautious steps downstream, lengthening more line and trying to work myself into a better position. The fly made several passes in front of the fish, but the trout refused to take it.

With another wave, the sentry on the bridge caught my attention and in a subdued voice asked me, "What fly are you using?" I told him. He said, "Tie on a number fourteen Mallard Quill, and if you have one, tie on a Leadwing Coachman as a dropper." I nodded my head in approval, sat down on an old deadfall, and honored his wishes. I waded back into position and sent my pair of flies on their mission. They touched the water about a dozen feet above the fish. Just as the flies began to swing, I felt a strong pull. My reel screeched and the fish made a run downstream that had me out on the bank following him. It was give and take for ten minutes before the large brown rolled over on his side. I slipped the net under him and lifted the fish out of the water. He was eighteen inches, all body, with a small head. The fish had taken the Mallard Quill solidly in the corner of his mouth.

I looked up towards the bridge where my grinning conspirator was now giving me the thumbs up sign. "A beautiful fish," he said. "Bring him up here; I would like to see him."

After we both admired the trout, I thanked him for his advice. We talked for two hours, exchanging flies and swapping notes. His flies were almost entirely wet, all tied in various sizes and were neatly placed on felt leaves in an old, leather fly book. Some of the oldest flies were tied on gut, snelled, but so beautifully tied that he was reluctant to discard them. Brittleness had doomed them, but the memories remained.

Harry's early Catskill angling days were spent on the upper Neversink, at Claryville, with Pop and Ed Sens. It was there that he learned to "spit" wet flies (as he termed it), usually in pairs under the surface.

It was also on the Neversink that Ed Sens created some of his fly patterns that became well known to fishermen in the nineteen-thirties and forties. Years later, when I met Ed, I was fortunate enough to inspect some of his flies and discuss different tying methods with him. Both Harry and Ed had vivid recollections of their angling days on the Neversink. They spoke of Ed Hewitt and the old sage, Herman Christian, who, they insisted, could fish wet flies with the best of them.

Our conversation on the bridge was one of many we would have in the years that followed. We fished quite regularly, mostly Catskill and Adirondack waters, and spent a considerable amount of time on the Battenkill River that flows through Vermont into New York State.

Angling pressure on the 'Kill in the nineteen-fifties was considerably less than it is today, and it was not uncommon to take brown trout, fifteen to twenty inches in length, on a fly. I have seen fish, taken on bait, that went upwards of five pounds and better, in the very deep holes. Roy Brown's tackle shop was a favorite meeting place on the river. You could share fishing experiences with other anglers and have a bite to eat. Just across the road was the Spring Hole, a camp shared by a group of intrepid anglers from the Albany area.

Lee Wulff also owned a house along the Battenkill. Harry and I would stop in on occasion and visit. As busy as Lee was editing film and working on projects, he always had time to chat for a while.

Sunday mornings were always a pleasure. We would drive over to Pop Tripp's house for an old-fashioned breakfast of blueberry pancakes, eggs, bacon, ham, sausages, and plenty of scalding hot coffee. Pop, dressed in a white apron and chef's hat, cooked over an old wood stove with his gray, tiger cat friend, Mr. Murphy, presiding over the feast. They were great times, on a great river, during a great era.

In addition to brown trout, the headwaters of the Battenkill held an ample supply of native brook trout. We enjoyed fishing for these dimpling fish where the river was shaded and the water always cooler on warm summer afternoons. It was a good excuse to avoid the hot, midday sun on the downriver, big water. That could wait until evening.

It was on one of those steamy, muggy afternoons, after hooking some small brookies, when Harry asked me if we might take a break and drive down to Orvis to pick up a new pair of scissors. He had misplaced or lost the pair on his vest and found it difficult to change flies. We headed for the tackle store.

At that time, Hardy made scissors that had a small pair of jaws at the tip of the blades for pinching on shot, trimming leaders, changing tippets, or tying on flies. The Hardy name was imprinted on one of the blades. Harry and I each bought one. Those scissors were invaluable over the years. They were efficient and, most of all, they stayed sharp.

I attached the scissors to my vest, and there they hung for years. I had fished the Atlantic salmon rivers of the

Canadian provinces, paddled canoes through northern Maine waters, fished who-knows-how-many miles of trout streams, and yet my little pair of scissors never failed me.

At least twenty years had gone by and Harry, who was now in his eighties, was forced to slow down because of his health. His fishing trips were fewer and fewer, but on occasion he would like to get together on an accessible piece of water, make a few casts, and sit down to reminisce. I always enjoyed accommodating him.

One evening, while fishing a small stream alone for native brook trout, I came upon a huge pool, deep and dark. There were trout rising, dimpling, and taking in small midges as they drifted down the lazy current. Deciding to change to a smaller fly for the midging trout, I sat down, adjusted the tippet, and tied on the small fly. On the final snip, I noticed that my scissors had parted; the two rings sat separately on my thumb and index finger. The pin had fallen out. I finished fishing the pool, took a few small brook trout, and with darkness settling in, called it a day.

When I arrived home in the evening, I was notified of Harry's passing that afternoon. One-half of my scissors dangled from my vest, swinging like a pendulum, side to side.

Fishing the riffles with a pair of wet flies.

The Quest

Chestnut Creek is deceiving. The road through the small Catskill village of Grahamsville twists and turns, following a small brook that flows into the Rondout Reservoir. In springtime, swollen waters reach over their banks, cleansing away the gray weariness of winter. In summer, the creek moves at a slower pace, low, warm, and uninviting. To a fisherman, it is a sign of despair. Do not be misled. Prior to entering the reservoir, a discharge of cold water from another reservoir joins the Chestnut. The mouth of the river creates ideal habitat for big brown trout. On occasion I also have hooked wild brookies and a few nice lake trout.

In the Catskills the biggest trout are found in reservoirs. Bank fishermen and trollers account for most of the catches. The trollers I have met are methodical and ingenious in their methods, trolling at various speeds and depths. They keep boats on several reservoirs, choosing which one to fish based upon local reports, and they row manually because regulations forbid any form of motorized propulsion. Fishing from dawn until dusk, they release trout in the two to eight-pound class, searching for ten-pound fish or better. As far as I know, their record is fourteen pounds. They swear they have hooked and lost larger fish. I believe them. I tip my hat to these sweepers of the deep. They work hard.

Early one season, my wife and I caught a few browns up to four pounds, trolling Gray Ghosts and other streamers just under the surface. We didn't catch many trout, but proved that it could be done. We probably should have done more of this flat-line trolling with flies, but could not refuse the call of our rivers. Perhaps in the future, more intrepid fish-

ermen gifted with strong rowing arms will pursue this venture to their advantage. It should be done early season, just
after ice-out when the fish are on top.

All fishermen dream of hooking large fish. Fly fishermen
are no exception. They have visions of a huge trout clamp-
ing down on wisps of feathers floating the current on a
favorite pool. Any fly tyer will tell you that each fly coming
out of a vise conjures up thoughts of big fish.

Years ago, when gray hair on my head was still unthink-
able, I wished that some day the big-fish gods would be
favorable and grant me a five-pound Catskill trout, taken on
a dry fly. My wish was made in wholesome, sporting spirit,
not as an obsession. I suppose this quest is similar to that of
a hopeful Catskill deer hunter. In these mountains, white-
tails are plentiful, but really big racks are few and far
between. For myself, I am grateful for the bounty of venison
harvested over the years, although I have to admit most of
the deer taken sported small racks—spikehorns to eight-
pointers. Wouldn't it be nice if some day that big ten or
twelve-pointer with a wide spread made an appearance! You
betcha!

Every once in a while the urge comes over me to search
for *the* fish. Few local rivers, save the big Delaware, hold
numbers of trout in excess of five pounds. I chose the reservoirs as my best bet. The problem, where waters are deep
and vast, is trying to find a big, feeding trout and then make
him come to the fly. Spring and fall offer the best opportunities for large fish: spring, because water temperature is
right, food is abundant, and fish will move into the shallows
where rivers enter the lake; fall, because trout begin to
school in preparation for the spawning run. The only draw-
back with fall fishing is the unpredictable reservoir water
levels from year to year. Regardless of the season, taking a
big fish requires opportunity, observation, and persistence.

Twenty years ago I put a boat in the Rondout Reservoir,
near the mouth of the Chestnut. It offered me easier access to

Big wet flies on heavy irons.

the more productive water, and fishing regulations were more relaxed then. I would row my boat to a jutting point of land that extended to the mouth of the Chestnut, and, using a drag anchor, drift the edge of the current, casting wet flies down and across the length of the flow. When the float was completed, I would return to the upstream position and start over again. For a change of pace, I would sometimes fish down and across with a dry fly, using short floats.

It was six o'clock on a warm, June evening when I parked my little jeep on top of a hill, off the main road. Gathering my rod, tackle, and oars, I hiked down the steep incline to where my boat was chained to a giant hemlock. A mouse shuffled beneath the leaves as I searched for the lock. Another one scattered when I turned the boat over. These little homesteaders are great opportunists, finding comfort in the insulation under the boat seats. I've tried to evict these tiny squatters, but they refuse to relinquish their territory. Sometimes they join me while I'm rowing, coming out from beneath the seats to stretch their little legs, and more than once I swear they've giggled when I've lost fish.

On this humid evening, a thick mist rose from the colder waters of the creek, creating an enchanting, but eerie quality to the setting. At dusk, a pack of coon dogs, maybe Red Bone or Blue Ticks, began howling behind the northwest tree line. Lengthening evening shadows, baying hounds, and a cold fog rising over a jutting moor reminded me of another, legendary moor across the sea. Some night, while listening to the whine of my creaky oarlocks, I fully expect to see a tall gentleman wearing a deerstalker hat appear through the shifting mist with a doctor as companion.

A fish broke forty feet across from me, then another just downstream of it. I eased the boat into position and drifted a wet fly past the lower fish. He took it and immediately moved into the faster water. Several minutes later I netted, and released, a fourteen-inch brown trout.

The fish further upstream remained undisturbed, and continued feeding on the surface. I saw the dorsal fin and tail as he porpoise-rolled at the edge of the heavy water. I removed the wet fly from my tippet and attached a Hair Wing Coachman dry fly. The fly landed a dozen feet above the fish. He rolled again. The Coachman disappeared and I felt the trout's head twisting, a throbbing motion. Then, with a powerful surge of the tail, he bolted downstream. I knew I had a good fish on. There were bursts of runs and a flurry of rolls. I eased him into the quiet lake water. Minutes later the fight was over. I slipped the landing net beneath him and lifted, surprised by the weight. "Good Lord," I said to myself, "after decades of dreaming, could this be it?" I fumbled for the scale in my vest and measured him—twenty-four inches of gleaming silver. I weighed him. The spring scale read five pounds, one ounce. I sank back against the seat of the boat and took a long, deep breath.

At home, later in the evening, I presented the big trout to my wife. She stared at the fish, then at me. "This is the one!" she said. "Yes," I answered. She replied, "After all these years. I think you should have him mounted." Realizing that this was my five minutes of fame in life, I agreed. The next afternoon, I noticed a small vase filled with wildflowers on my fly tying desk.

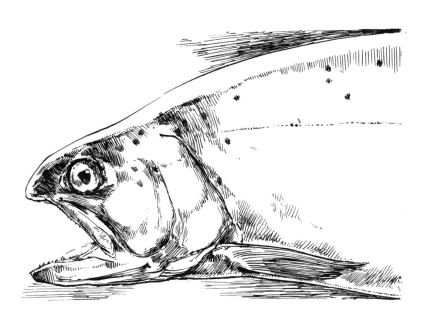

Blueberry Trout

August was hot. Morning dew hung heavily over a field of wildflowers and patches of goldenrod. The big rivers, whose banks overflow in springtime, were lonely, displaying a desolate avenue of stones. Trout feeding on abundant insect life weeks earlier had vanished into deeper pools and cooler water.

Down in the valley, colorful handwritten signs on telephone poles advertised Saturday night auctions and church suppers. Family-owned farm stands displayed wooden crates overflowing with vegetables and fresh fruit. The sights and aromas were sensory signals reminding me that it was time to gather blueberries. These are not the small, low bush berries found on the barren tops of mountains near home, but the succulent, high bush berries growing in damp abandoned pastures.

The following morning I assembled the simple equipment needed: a large pail with a lid that fitted easily into my pack basket, a length of rope for securing the cover, a wide-brimmed hat to protect my head from a hot sun, and a pair of below-the-knee rubber boots. A cane fly rod and willow creel were stashed behind the front seat of the jeep.

I parked on a shady knoll, at the end of an old logging road, next to a hidden spring that seeped from a bluestone ledge. A small rock pool, moss-covered with age, was built there years ago when this was a working farm. All of that is gone now, abandoned, giving testament to the harsh, Catskill winters and rock-strewn earth.

Before beginning my journey through the meadow I pulled out a small metal cup, sampled the ice cold spring water, filled my jug, and placed it in the bottom of the basket.

Nature was kind. It was a good year for berries. I share these sweet fruits with black bears. Evidence lies near a heavy thicket—a pile of fresh scat layered with unripe, green apples, blueberries, and more green apples. The first bushes I came to were filled with fruit. A whitish chalk covered the outer, blue skin. I was selective, picking only the ripe blueberries, unlike the messy bears that, short on etiquette, strip the leaves, berries, and twigs bare. The first mouthful exploded with the taste of sweet nectar. In one respect I agreed with the sloppy bears, letting the juices drip from my mouth. My fingers were blue.

I moved through this patch quickly, working my way to a seepage at the bottom of a pasture, where in better years the choice berries grow best. As I crossed a small brook, a ruffed grouse bolted from cover. Reaction was swift. My imaginary double barrel followed "old ruff" above the tops of the willows. I got him! (I never miss in make-believe situations.)

As I neared the edge of the pasture, I smiled. The bushes were swollen with blueberries. I was in no hurry. Being careful to pick and choose, I listened to the tinkling of the berries dropping into the metal cup. It only took moments to fill. I transferred the contents into the larger pail, repeated this several times, and then rested, making myself comfortable on a fallen log beneath an old maple tree. Lazy clouds floated slowly across a pale, summer sky.

I filled the cup with spring water from the moisture-covered jug, and sipped. Looking across the pasture, I reflected on the paradox of hard times when simple pleasures were so abundant. On a small hill were remnants of a stone foundation, surrounded by old lilac bushes stubbornly clinging to life.

Listening carefully, I could hear the excited voices of yesterday's laughing children, stumbling over pails of berries as they hurry from bush to bush. A young voice

A late summer monarch.

cries out, "Come here, quick! Look what I've found!"
Another voice exclaims, "Over here! I've found more!"

I'm sure there were more than a few milkers here, plus a
team of horses and cackling hens scratching endlessly
around the yard. Rough, hand-hewn timbers from an old
barn still stand, framing this mental picture.

A deer snorted behind me, stomping impatiently, breaking into my daydream. I turned my head and watched as a
small doe sniffed the air. I rose from the log, reached for my
cup, and continued to pick berries. It didn't take long to fill
the large pail. Finished, I tied the lid to the handles so the
berries would not spill and placed it in my pack basket.
Despite the heavy weight on sagging shoulders, the trek
back through the pasture was worth the effort.

Several minutes away from where I parked, an old wood-
en bridge spans a small brook not more than a dozen feet in
width. The waters are well shaded and cold. Brook trout are

native here. Never stocked, they are glacier-age fish, small and dark in color. Casting a fly over these little gems is part of my blueberry pilgrimage.

The rod is short, six feet in length. A small number sixteen Hair Wing Coachman dry fly is tied to a 5x tippet. My low boots are more than adequate for wading in the shallow waters. The largest pool is no more than three feet in depth, others much less.

I hiked a short way upstream until I reached a small pool with an undercut bank. A low side-cast put the fly on top of the shallow current. As it drifted near the bank, a fish rose for the fly. A subtle twitch of the rod was all that was needed. He was hooked. I navigated the fish away from the cover, and a small brook trout came to the net. I slipped him into my willow basket filled with green ferns and repeated this little feat one more time. I was satisfied—two plump natives were enough.

A beaver pond squaretail.

At home the ritual continued. There were berries to be washed, pie crusts to be made, and two brook trout to be seasoned for the skillet. That evening, my wife and I dined on brook trout, crisp salad, and wine, followed by generous slices of warm, blueberry pie. Scoops of vanilla ice cream were optional. We saved an ample supply of blueberries for breakfast pancakes and froze the rest.

On a cold winter's morning the scents of August permeate the kitchen air. My thoughts slip back to an overgrown pasture, white clouds, the hum of summer insects, and rising fish ... blueberry trout.

Autumn Landlocks

Nature has her way of shifting an angler's mood. A summer of trout fishing on Catskill rivers becomes increasingly difficult. The larger trout are extremely wary after a season of pounding, and any productive fly fishing will occur either in the morning or late evening. A fly line, no matter how gently cast, scatters fish in the warm, still water pools.

During a lull, I find comfort on the bank beneath the shade of a large tree, drifting back against its trunk, absorbing summer's sights and sounds. Further down the bank, a clump of purple loosestrife seeps out of a bed of dry cobblestones. A monarch butterfly settles upon its flowers. Thoughts slip back to a large, northern lake where a salmon has just swirled and missed my streamer fly. As the concentric rings disappear, another monarch, migrating south, drifts over the tip of my rod. This scene is replayed in my mind until a scurrying flock of mergansers awakens me from my daydream. Summer is waning. It is time to think of salmon.

Swallows depart the eastern Catskills by the twenty-fifth of August. During the evening hours the loud drone of katydids wail a song of inevitable frost. Further to the north an early smattering of red maple leaves clutter a pool on a half-dry riverbed. Landlocked salmon drift towards the mouths of brooks, waiting for the fall rains to raise water levels. All summer they have fed heavily on smelt in the deep-water lakes of northern New York and New England.

On first arrival these freshwater cousins of the Atlantic sea-going salmon are steel blue and bright silver, with the familiar black St. Andrew's crosses filtering down their sides. After weeks of lying in shallow-water pools, they will turn a reddish-brown color, stale in appearance. Fresh fish will continue to arrive in larger numbers as spawning season approaches. They are very similar to *Salmo Salar* in their habits, only on a miniature scale. If there is one trait that the two fish have in common, it is their temperamental moodiness. They will lie motionless, as if cast in bronze, mesmerized by the comforting currents, never far from deep-water sanctuaries. At times, with a harmonious sweep of tail and fins, a fish may launch itself forward and upward, heaving water into a spray. The fish re-enters and makes a tour of the pool, halting to rest on a lie it occupied moments before. Then, the fish again becomes a sculpture, seemingly oblivious to the watery world around it.

These are trying times for the salmon angler, but to those who understand salmon this is accepted as a matter of fact. The angler knows that at any given moment a salmon may rise from his lie and strike the moving fly. More often than not, the strike comes unannounced and is followed by a heavy pull labeled with definitive authority. Long runs, successive leaps, and head-shaking follows, which brings the angler back time and time again.

Salmon fishing is a casting game, and at times quite strenuous, particularly on open water. Strong gusts of fall winds whip flies inches away from the angler's face. Hours of casting, intermittent changes of flies, and different retrieving speeds are all a fisherman can offer. These adjustments can still lead to rejection, and much success depends on the whims of the fish. This is salmon fishing, and a true salmon angler must be born with the right temperament. I have seen good trout fishermen who are successful because they have something more tangible to deal with—namely, feeding fish—go to pieces because they cannot raise a salmon. This is not inability, but rather a failure to adjust a mindset. There is a different set of rules in this type of fishing. Patience, perseverance, and casting are the keys to success.

Reassurance is resurrected when a school of fresh-run landlocks is seen slicing through the waves and sweeping over sandbars. Fresh from the depths and traveling, they are vulnerable to taking a fly. A streamer cast ahead of the fish is stripped quickly through the incoming waves, followed by a boil, then a double-boil, and finally a strong pull, tightening the line. The endless hours of casting culminate in pure joy when five pounds of silver are lying in the net.

Quiet lake waters are not favorable for the fisherman. An angler hopes for windswept waters because salmon are more active in turbulent water. Any abrupt change in the lake surface can put fish on the move.

Morning and evening are generally the best times to cast for fall landlocks. New waves of fish, and activity among stale salmon, are at their height during these hours. You may be greeted by a silent porpoise-roll or the resounding smack as the salmon's body slaps the surface, not unlike the tail of a beaver when it strikes water. Although this is the most

Wind, waves, and a lady with her salmon.

opportune time to be on the water, it does not mean that fish cannot be taken during the day. On the contrary, many of my fine catches have been made between nine o'clock in the morning and four in the afternoon. Wind and waves play an important role. I know of an Adirondack lake where you can set your watch on the wind coming up at 9:00 AM. It stimulates the fish to move to the edge of the gravel bars. Cloud cover and rain can also be helpful, even on quiet waters. Raindrops pelting the surface can cause enough agitation to put fish in a striking mood.

My wife and I experienced a rain-soaked day that proved to be one of those days that we will never forget. We arrived at eight o'clock in the morning with low, dark clouds hovering over the distant mountains. Within a very short time, perhaps ten or fifteen minutes, the first raindrops appeared. Then, the skies opened and it poured, sheets of rain coming in hard from the northeast. Accompanying winds pushed our fly lines well off the mark. The heavy downpours seemed to find the smallest openings in our rain gear. Even with tight cuffs, water would seep down our arms soaking our sleeves. I glanced over at Lisa. She nodded in return. Our thoughts were the same. Should we continue to cast, or should we pack our gear and leave? We signaled our intent: "one more cast."

As I lengthened line for my final throw, I saw a salmon roll at the mouth of the brook. A number eight Barnes Special landed in front of the swirl. I felt a sharp pull. Several minutes later, Lisa slipped the net under a four-pound landlocked salmon. Within the next hour, the heavy downpour notwithstanding (strange how the weather didn't bother us now), we caught five more salmon, all three to five pounds. Three of these fish were silver and bright; the remainder were stale, reddish-brown in color. All the males had hooked kypes. That morning we had done very well.

Very often, salmon show a preference for a particular fly. Color and size can mean the difference between mediocre and good fishing. Granted, a fly that is fished often enough and with confidence will usually perform well, but salmon can possess an uncanny ability to choose a fly with the fastidiousness of a world-class wine taster. Some flies will produce well for a while, then lose favor. Then there are those flies that have proven themselves over time, and it would be wise for a new angler to concentrate on these patterns. It is my personal opinion that, at least for fall landlocks, the color yellow has much appeal either in the entire fly or in part. The Dark and Light Tigers, along with the Mickey Finn, Sanborn, Magog Smelt, and the Barnes Special in sizes six and eight, are fine choices. Too bulky a tie causes the fly to ride along the surface, so these flies should be tied sparsely to allow them to sink. The standard salmon streamers—Gray Ghost, Nine-Three, Supervisor, and other smelt imitations— are also fine flies, although I find them more effective after ice-out in the spring of the year, when salmon are on a ravenous feed.

One of the problems with a tinsel-bodied salmon streamer is that the teeth of the fish can tear the body apart. A fly tyer can create a sturdier body by picking up the slack on the oval tinsel rib. To do this, before tying off the oval tinsel, pull it straight down near the eye and hold it. Now, with your left thumb and forefinger, twist the oval from the back of the hook and along the shank moving forward toward the head in a clockwise direction. It is the same movement as winding a watch. Keep pulling down with your right hand as you go. You will now have picked up all of the slack. Tie it off and lacquer the body.

Small wet flies, both trout and salmon patterns, are also effective. These are especially successful when landlocks are porpoise-rolling. As with streamer flies, there are wet fly patterns that are more reliable than others. I recall several years ago when a black Woolyworm, minus the red tail and tied on a number eight hook, was the last word on catching fish on our home waters. For two years the fly could do no wrong. In fact, its success was rather remarkable. Then, for some reason the fly lost favor. Success after that was minimal.

The Gold Ribbed Hare's Ear, in sizes eight through twelve, is another good pattern. Some fishermen I know tie this pattern in nymph form and do quite well fishing it with a slow retrieve.

Atlantic salmon patterns—the Rusty Rat, Ross Special, Silver Gray, and the Butt patterns—are equally effective tied in sizes six through ten.

Fall winds blowing across open waters create casting problems for an angler. Tackle should be adequate enough to push a fly line through the wind and turn over the larger flies. The longer rod can be an asset when wading deep water. An eight-and-one-half or nine-foot rod is a dependable choice. The rod must be light in the hand, an important feature if one expects to cast for several hours at a time. A heavy rod causes fatigue, which is physically hard enough, but mentally distracting to a point where fishing is no longer enjoyable. The seven and eight weight-forward tapers are ideal for casting larger flies. They also lend a hand when reaching for the extra foot if needed.

The idea that the only purpose of a fly reel is to store fly line is nonsense. The reel should be large enough to store line and backing comfortably. It only takes the loss of one good fish that ran out of line to prove the point. The fly reel should be well lubricated and have an adjustable drag. Set the drag on the light side, just enough to prevent overrun. This can be critical when fish are in close. The sight of a net can revive a fish, especially when it's a salmon who is not quite ready. A sudden surge pulling against a tight drag can leave a flyless leader drifting in the breeze.

A nine-foot leader, tapered to a six or eight-pound test, is a good choice for salmon. Use a stiff leader, especially the butt section, which should be attached with a needle nail-knot. The leader should be inserted through the fly line, then finished with a nail-knot and varnished. This prevents the knot from jamming. Also, be sure to cut the knots close on the leader sections if you make your own. The ends will catch in the guides if they are too long. Should this happen when playing a fish, simply reverse the rod so the reel is top-side. The line and leader will slide against the rod, not the guides.

A quality net large enough to land a salmon is an asset to any angler. Wind and waves can make landing a fish difficult enough without compounding the problems by using a small, trout net. There are several competent ones on the market. I prefer a large, metal, triangular, collapsible net that has an extension handle. Folded, it is clipped to a ring on the back of a vest or jacket, out of the way. When a fish is ready, a quick twist unfolds the net and it is easily maneuvered into position.

With all gear in working order a salmon angler wades confidently into his favorite waters. The hours spent casting may catch the whim of a salmon, perhaps not today, but maybe tomorrow. Hope *does* spring eternal in the angler's heart.

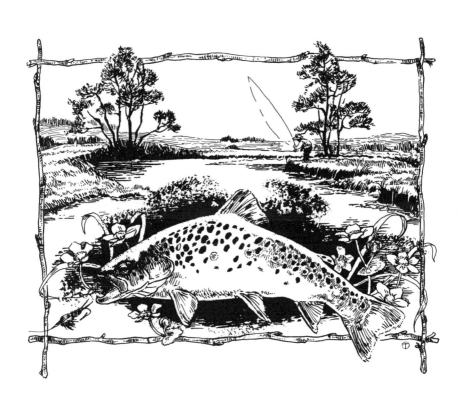

A Full Creel

Anglers spend a lifetime wading rivers, making plans, and devising all sorts of techniques to place a fly in the corner of a fish's mouth. If the fisherman takes angling seriously, he is usually rewarded, and in the process becomes quite proficient at his craft. As the years pass, aggressiveness begins to wane and a sense of satisfaction is derived purely from being at the river's edge. Enjoyment of the sport branches out far beyond what occurs beneath the water's surface.

Back in the "old" days, I observed a milkman driving a single horse-drawn wagon on a lonely cobblestone street in the early dawn hours. The old gray horse, marred with canker sores and hampered by a deep curvature of the back, plodded along with a slow rhythmic cadence, making his rounds with the familiarity only a postman can understand. At each appointed stop, without prodding from his master, the horse would automatically pause, then wait for the driver to return from his delivery. Maybe it was the clinking of the empty bottles that gave the move-ahead signal, but without any visible sign from the driver the horse would begin the slow, monotonous gait once the milkman was seated. The process was repeated over and over again. The horse wore a pair of leather blinders that limited the peripheral vision of both eyes. Rarely did I see him shift his tired head from side to side, save an occasional snort or a headshake to rid himself of bothersome flies. His was a straight-ahead world.

We live in a frenetic world crammed with deadlines and pressures, culminating in the need for instant gratification.

Nothing is done in moderation, and there is little time left for reflection. Sadly, some of these less desirable traits of modern day society have crept their way into the "contemplative" world of angling. Like the horse drawing the milk wagon, the eyes of many anglers today are focused straight ahead on water, and water alone. Moving at breakneck speed they take the workplace with them to the river. In many respects, I feel sorry for those anglers who fail to see the joys associated with angling.

I know of an intimate, little river where there are small, native brook trout hidden beneath undercut banks. I can see them dart from cover to midstream, grabbing a morsel of food and retreating back to the safety of their hidden world. The spongy moss banks are strewn with aged, green hemlocks. Old apple trees lean over lichen-covered stone walls that disappear into a tangle of wild grapes. Late summer and fall are good times to fish here. The headwaters are fed by cool springs that give sanctuary to both fish and men. Evening, after the sun disappears behind the western mountains, is a good time to put a dry fly on these little mountain pools. Small trout poke their chins out to bump these little feathered offerings. Sometimes I am victorious, but more often than not I find my fly embedded in some underwater root or sunken branch.

This little corner of my world abounds with wildlife. I see wild turkeys when I am sitting on the bank retying a leader or changing a fly. They move down from the hardwood ridges to roost in the thick hemlocks at dusk. I can hear them shuffling through the leaves, feeding as they travel across the forest floor foraging on grubs and insects. Subtle little grunts and clucks are followed by the intermittent scratching of leaves.

I once saw a black bear sitting down with legs apart, stuffing himself on green apples, leaves, dry grass, and anything else his front paws would scoop into his mouth. For want of a better view of this orgy, I decided to move closer to the stone wall. With a few yards to go, my foot snapped a dry branch hidden under leaves. The bear's head swung in my direction. The nose at the point of his brown muzzle lifted into the wind. With astonishing speed he was up and over the wall heading for higher ground. I was amazed at the unbelievable silence with which he made his exit.

A river full of memories.

Whitetail deer are constant companions. More than once as I moved upstream with a dry fly I have seen a fawn lying motionless on the bank. I am sure they spotted me long before I saw them. I knew the doe was not far away, hidden in the shadows. I kept moving slowly at my normal pace, fishing upstream until I was well out of sight.

One evening, I was joined by a young, spikehorn buck feeding on wild grasses. He grazed unaware as I netted several small brook trout. He eventually drifted off into the lengthening shadows, his white tail wavering from side to side.

There was a day in the spring of a year that I took my five-year-old son Paul fishing with me. I would place him in a homemade pack frame and seat him on my back. When I hooked a trout, I would give him the rod and let him play the fish. During one of our short breaks, he spied a wood-cock sitting beneath some willows, with several young ones milling around the nest site. He walked over and carefully reached down, placing one of the young woodcock in the palm of his hand. He uttered some loving words that only a child can say to a little new-found friend, and then gently returned him to the brood. The mother woodcock tolerated the intrusion and sat there, tall beak extending downward. We watched as she stood up and moved the entire brood to another willow thicket. We heard little peeps evaporating into the heavy cover.

There is a trout stream behind my home. It is a small tributary, not a primary spawning stream, but in the fall of the year a sprinkling of brown trout filter into the headwa-ters and perform their annual ritual. In the springtime this rite is repeated again, this time by a few migrating rainbow trout.

It was an overcast, drizzly day in early May. A few Hendricksons struggled to dry their waterlogged wings. I picked up an old cane rod, put on my rain gear, and walked the bank in search of a rising fish. Water dripped from rain-soaked branches as I reached Split Rock Pool. I paused to wipe my fogged eyeglasses. When I replaced them, my eyes focused on the tail of the pool where I noticed a flash of sil-ver. I crept forward a little further and concealed myself behind several low-hanging hemlock branches. I parted them and took a closer look. There, on the clean gravel, were two large rainbows exercising their courtship. The flashing motion I had seen was the female fish on her side fanning gravel from the newly formed redd. The male fish, aggressive but patient, remained at her side. The cloudy day cast no shadows, and from my hidden position, I marveled as these two wild fish followed the natural urge. Then, with the shyness of one who suddenly happens upon a lovers' tryst, I slipped away carefully, without a sound. I would fish another day.

A perceptive angler is wise enough to accept what the day will give him. He will travel home with a light heart, richer for the day's experiences. His creel will always be full.

Appendix

Getting Started

The first requirement of any angler is to purchase a New York State fishing license and to familiarize him or herself with a booklet of regulations that comes with the license. Regulations vary from river to river with regards to the size and limits of trout allowed. I also recommend the acquisition of a New York City Watershed fishing permit, available free of charge. The information for this permit is also in the New York State booklet of regulations.

The new fishermen, like us before them, will wade their first river with enthusiasm and anticipation. Rest assured, they will be confused and ask endless questions of fellow anglers, until one day, somehow, this beautiful puzzle begins to make sense. Or does it? In the final analysis, the realization will come that it is *they* who are hooked.

The new angler anxious to discover fly fishing should visit the Catskill Flyfishing Center and Museum located on Old Route 17 in Livingston Manor. The history of Catskill fly fishing starts there. Everyone and everything pertaining to fly angling in these mountains is condensed within its walls. It sets the tone for a sport steeped in history.

Someone interested in learning how to fly fish will ask, "How do I get started?" Throughout this book, I have given pointers on tackle, flies, and equipment used under various fishing conditions that have worked for me. Ideally, it would be grand if you knew someone who had years of experience and was willing to show you the way, a streamside mentor if you will.

I often hear the remark, "Oh, I could never do that. It would take me forever to learn to cast the way that you do." Fly fishing is no black art full of mystery and magic potions, as some would have you believe, but any worthwhile endeavor does requires practice. Guidance, balanced tackle, and practice will have you casting well enough to catch fish in a relatively short time. And remember: in fly fishing, where the line puts the lure out (not as in bait casting or spinning, where the weight of the lure throws out the line) there is no room for, "Well, my equipment's good enough to learn with." That statement lacks good judgment. You are doomed from the beginning. Good tackle is necessary for good casting, and good casting will improve your chances of catching fish. Every time you wade the river you will learn something new. Choose your tackle well, take your time, and enjoy the experience!

For those who have no angling friends, do not despair; there are alternatives. Throughout the Catskills, there are several fly fishing schools with "on the water" learning as well as classroom instruction. The costs of these schools vary, so it would be prudent to check around and find one that fits your budget.

Another avenue to pursue is Trout Unlimited, a national organization dedicated to preserving quality trout fishing. There are several chapters in the Catskills. You will find the members to be congenial and helpful. Many of the chapters conduct their own casting clinics and fly tying classes. You can become a member by contacting the national headquarters: Trout Unlimited, P.O. Box 1335, Merrifield, VA 2216-9801, Tel: 1.800.834.2419. For information about the local chapters of Trout Unlimited, call 703.284.9418.

In the late 1800s when Theodore Gordon fingered flies imported from Great Britain, the dry fly in the United States was about to undergo a transformation. The imported fly patterns were in color, size, and soft hackle quality befitting the slow-moving rivers and streams of England. Gordon recognized this and pioneered the style of Catskill flies we use today, which meant hackle stiff enough to float a fly on fast water. Fly tyers Roy Steenrod, Herman Christian, Reub Cross, Harry and Elsie Darbee, and Walt and Winnie Dette continued to tie flies using the same basic principle. Today, there is a coterie of fly tyers in the Catskills that adhere to these traditions. They make their headquarters a stone's throw from the Beaver Kill River. The address is: Catskill Fly Tyers Guild, P.O. Box 663, Roscoe, NY 12776-0663.

There are excellent accommodations to be found throughout the region. Bed and Breakfasts, lodges, motels, and campsites are readily available. Towns like Roscoe, Livingston Manor, Margaretville, Hunter, and Phoenicia cater to fishermen. In fact, the Phoenicia Library houses an upstairs room devoted to fly fishing. There are plenty of tackle shops to aid both the novice and expert fishermen alike. Many offer information on fishing maps, fly hatches, water conditions, and guide services.

Another major source of information is the New York State Department of Environmental Conservation, Bureau of Fisheries, 625 Broadway, Albany, New York 12233-4753.